Lost Between the Extensivity / Intensivity Exchange

Warren Neidich

Diagrams of the Mind

Sven-Olov Wallenstein

Latin diagramma, figure, from Greek, a figure worked out by lines, plan, from diagraphein, to mark out, delineate: dia-, dia- + graphein, to write; see gerbh- in Indo-European roots.

(The American Heritage Dictionary of the English Language)

I

In the landscape of contemporary artistic and critical operations, by which we can understand those practices that seem increasingly difficult to separate from theoretical work, as well as those theories that refuse the state of merely abstract reflections on already existing practices, the diagram—a writing or drawing "<u>dia</u>," "through," a schema that is worked out or traversed by lines that are not only physical but also immaterial, lines of flight as well as lines that constitute dead ends and machines of capture—has become an eminently useful concept. From visual arts to architecture, from philosophy to theories of organization, the diagram has escaped the condition of something merely graphic, a representation of a set of relations established elsewhere, and has become more akin to an instrument of thinking, or even something that engenders thought itself.[1] In Warren Neidich's "Diagrammatic Drawings" we find a distinct take on this theme, a way to use the diagrammatic mode of thinking in order to connect areas of research, discourse, and practice, which in the contemporary division of labor between on the one hand the sciences, on the other hand the humanities and the arts, seem destined to either remain deaf to each other, or produce the fantasy of asymmetrical reductions and appropriations. Bringing together concepts from neurology and the life sciences, political philosophy and aesthetic theory, theories of immaterial labor and post-Fordist production, Neidich creates a maze of concepts and connections that may at first sight seem bewildering, and even more so since he explores them not just as theoretical concepts, each located within their particular sphere, but as physical and corporeal zones that we can and indeed do inhabit, and that we traverse in the most minute of our everyday activities. But in doing so, he suggests that the transversal activity of the artist is a highly productive way of transgressing such limits, not in order to simply undo them—which most

often means that one domain overtakes the other—but to produce certain resonances and encounters, captures and assemblages that extract a power from each domain in order to project it into a new sphere. Philosophy, science, and art, Deleuze and Guattari claim in the final collaborative work <u>What is philosophy?</u>, each have their distinct properties and procedures—philosophy constructs concepts, science establishes functions, and art tears perceptions and affections away from the subject in order to elevate them into "percepts" and "affects," composites that have their own temporality and a proper way of "conserving" experiences in a virtual state—they are parallel activities none of which is inferior or superior to the others. But as three distinct modes of approaching "chaos," they also extract things from each other, they discover zones of indistinction, and it may be the task of all three to reflect—in a way that at a certain moment must suspend the securities and professional assurances of each—on such unforeseeable encounters. It is to such encounters that the practice of "diagrammatic drawing" may be related, in marking limits, thresholds, and breaks, but also establishing connections and allowing remote areas to communicate; it delves into a peculiar potential of the diagram that has attracted the attention not only of practitioners within the visual arts, but also philosophers and social scientists.

II

The word "diagram" seems indeed to have entered current thinking about art, architecture, and the visual/spatial arts through the influence of Deleuze, and particularly his book on Foucault (although the concept had already been used extensively both by Deleuze himself and in his collaborative work with Guattari, as we will see),[2] which picked up and extended a few seemingly off-hand remarks in Foucault's <u>Discipline and Punish</u>, which describe the relations of power in Bentham's plan for a Panopticon prison as a "diagram." In his analysis of the carceral and disciplinary techniques of the late 18th century, Foucault stresses that we should not see the diagram as a merely geometrical entity, and thus as connected to any particular form of architectural or spatial shape, but as a more abstract way

1.   The division between mere representation and the capacity to engender thought was of course never clear-cut, and the current extended use of the idea of the diagram may be seen as an actualization of possibilities that were there from the start, in the first Greek experiments with representation through graphs and letters. For a fascinating study of this topic, which traces the role of the—today no longer extant—diagrams in the texts of Greek mathematics, see REVIEL NETZ, **The Shaping of Deduction in Greek Mathematics** (Cambridge: Cambridge University Press, 1999), esp. chap. 1, "The lettered diagram."

2.   GILLES DELEUZE, **Foucault**, trans. Seán Hand (Minneapolis: University of Minnesota Press, 1988). Following Deleuze's book, the diagram has been used extensively in architectural theory; among the first to do so was Greg Lynn in a discussion of the work of Ben van Berkel, "Forms of Expression: The Proto-Functional Potential of Diagrams in Architectural Design," **El Croquis 72**, 1995. For a survey of recent uses, see the contributions in **Any 23**, "Diagram Work" (1998).

of ordering, a "type of location of bodies in space, of distribution of individuals in relation to one another, of hierarchical organization, of disposition of centers and channels of power, of definition of the instruments and modes of intervention of power, which can be implemented in hospitals, workshops, schools, prisons."[3] Or, formulated in the terminology that Deleuze and Guattari had already developed, the diagram can be understood as an "abstract machine" out of which relations of power emerge, and which is capable of assuming many different physical morphologies: it is the very condition of possibility of a stable physical order, but also that which envelops every order with a "becoming" of forces, a dimension of the virtual that makes all stable forms susceptible to change and disruption.

In the specific case of Bentham, the essential feature of the Panopticon diagram is its capacity to exert a maximal influence over a population by the minimal use of physical force, or, more precisely, to situate the prisoner within a permanent visibility that renders the application of power automatic. The Panopticon does this by transferring the active force to an "object" that thereby becomes individualized and "subjectivized" as the bearer of responsibility and locus of agency, which also means that the subject becomes endowed with a certain freedom. This is why Bentham can suggest that the Panopticon's outcome is a global increase in freedom and prosperity for all individuals: it invigorates economy, perfects health, and diffuses happiness throughout the body politic by installing a reflexive capacity in its subjects that renders them more productive.

Deleuze picks up on this—probably incidental—use of the term "diagram" in Foucault, and wittily connects it to a probably just as incidental use of the word "monogram" in Kant's <u>Critique of Pure Reason</u>. The Kantian monogram is used to characterize the temporal schema projected by the imagination— "an art concealed in the depths of the human soul, whose real modes of activity nature is hardly likely ever to allow us to discover, and to open to our gaze," Kant says—that ensures the passage from intelligibility to sensibility, or more precisely, from the categories of the understanding to the manifold of intuition. In this sense, the schema is not simply an empirical image, but, Kant proposes, "a product and, as it were monogram, of pure a priori imagination," and as such it is that "through which and in accordance with which images themselves first become possible."[4]

If the Kantian monogram is the purveyor of a certain unity of knowledge, the Foucauldian diagram (at least as developed by Deleuze) is rather what makes possible a manifold of practices, but also, through linking these practices together, that which transforms the fleeting and ephemeral events of discourse into stable "archives." Power can be understood as a diagram that molds and formalizes <u>matters</u> (the visible and the sayable, light and language, the two pure "Elements" of knowledge that Deleuze perceives as the Foucauldian sequels to reason and sensibility in Kant), and Deleuze likens it to a "cartography" coextensive with the social field, a mapping of those forces that traverse it, hold it together, but also provide it with a mobility and possibilities of reversals and disruptions. "A diagram is a map, or rather several superimposed maps," he writes,[5] the "the map of relations between forces, a map of destiny, or intensity, which [...] acts as a non-unifying immanent cause which is coextensive with the whole social field. The abstract machine is like the cause of the concrete assemblages that execute its relations; and these relations take place 'not above' but within the very tissue of the assemblages they produce."[6] If this machine, like Kantian schematism, can be said to be "blind", it is precisely in the sense that it is what makes us see and talk. Power is always actualized as a form (knowledge as structured into archives of light and language), otherwise it would remain in a pure virtual state, but inversely there would be no stable forms of knowledge unless they were immersed in relations of power. But if there is a mutual imbrication and "capture" between knowledge and power, this does not mean that they can be reduced to each other (a frequent misreading of Foucault is that he would say that knowledge is <u>nothing but</u> power)—in fact they remain irreducible to such an extent that they only communicate via a "non-place" or "disjunction," Deleuze suggests, which is why no assemblage of knowledge and power ever remains stable, but only exists in relation to those singularities that it attempts to capture and formalize.

Understood in this way, the diagram always has two sides. On the one hand, it integrates singular points by binding them in a curve or form in general; on the other hand it is an "emission" of singularities, and as such it is connected to a more profound Outside (<u>le Dehors</u>), a chaos or an "abstract hurricane" out of which it emerges through "draws" (<u>tirages</u>). This connection to the outside is what makes the diagram akin to philosophical thought, Deleuze suggests, which is why the act of thinking in itself constitutes an act of <u>resistance</u>: it is open

3.   MICHEL FOUCAULT, **Discipline and Punish**, trans. Alan Sheridan (London: Penguin, 1991), 205.

4.   IMMANUEL KANT, **Critique of Pure Reason**, trans. Norman Kemp-Smith (London: MacMillan, 1929), A 142/B 181. Further on, in the section on the Architectonic of Pure Reason, Kant makes use of the schema as a way to formulate the structural and not simply aggregative unity of reason, and distinguishes between a schema whose unification is "empirical" and only yields "technical unity," and one "which originates from an idea [and] serves as the basis of architectonic unity, that which we call science, whose schema contains the outline (**monogramma**) and the division of the whole into members in conformity with the idea" (A 833/B 861).

5.   DELEUZE, **Foucault**, 44.

6.   Ibid., 37.

to a formless future, to those virtual forces of becoming that constitute the "double" of history, but in this it is also and always a perilous act, with the risk of plunging us into mere chaos and death. Here, Deleuze notes, there is an encounter between Foucault and Heidegger, in that they both determine the possibility of thought through a fundamental relation to an Outside that is an un-grounding, that dispossesses consciousness.[7]

This aspect of formlessness and chaos is in fact reminiscent of an earlier use of the concept of the diagram in Deleuze, in his book on Francis Bacon, <u>Logique de la sensation</u>. The reading of Bacon's diagram prefigures the analysis of Foucault, but also points in a slightly different, although perhaps eventually complementary, direction. The context is the painter's resistance to photography: the ubiquity of the photographic image in contemporary culture, Bacon says, tends to fill the canvas with clichés and readymade forms. This means to reduce "sensation"—which is what Bacon attempts to capture, in a quest for a "logic" that (at least in Deleuze's reading) leads him to an incessant and critical dialogue with phenomenology and with Cézanne—to one singular level, and renders invisible those intensities and transformations that produce violent differences and spasms, sudden drops and increases in energy.[8] The problem for Bacon is thus never the empty canvas, as in the drama of reduction to flatness in modernist painting that had developed on the basis of Clement Greenberg's theories, where the reduction to the materiality of the support and the act of inscribing marks leads us from late modernist monochromes back to Mallarmé's pristine sheet of white paper that both calls upon and rejects the act of inscription. But neither is the issue to get "into" the painting—as in the opposite existential rhetoric of Harold Rosenberg, whose idea of "action" emphasized the other side of Abstract Expressionism, the self-creation of artist and artwork in the same ambivalent movement of expression. The painter, Deleuze says, is already inside, and fundamentally so against his will, because of the world of clichés, and the question he faces is rather how he, at a certain moment <u>before</u> painting, can get <u>out</u> of it. The strategy that Bacon adapts for attaining such a distance is to reintroduce a moment of chance in opposition to the merely "probable" (before we start to paint it is <u>probable</u> that we will reach certain forms, given what we have set as a task, for instance to paint a portrait), a chance that operates through the distribution of singular marks and allows the energy of the "figural" to erupt at a level situated below the form or the figurative.[9]

Bacon's technique is to use such randomly produced marks and stains of color in order to disfigure the all-too probable figure based on resemblance and representation, and Deleuze suggests that this should be seen as a "diagram," or a freely produced schema of possibilities that makes the initial and familiar form deviate from itself. The term appears occasionally in Bacon's conversations with David Sylvester (which are Deleuze's primary source), but its strategic importance seems to be an invention of Deleuze. The diagram is a "catastrophe" of the canvas, Deleuze proposes, in the etymological sense of an "overturning," an event that violently disrupts forms: "It is as if one would suddenly introduce a Sahara, a Sahara-zone, into the head; is if one introduced a rhinoceros skin, seen through a microscope."[10] These marks are non-signifying traits, attacks, or random inscriptions, and understood in terms of the diagram their task is to introduce new possibilities—indeed a chaos of sorts, but also the beginning of a "rhythm" that allows the painting to integrate, hysterically, its own <u>catastrophe</u>, as Deleuze puts it. The painter passes through a catastrophe in his use of the diagram, but in the process of retrieving the form, he discovers the Figure, liberated from the confines both of abstraction, where the hand is subordinated to a higher signification and an "optical" order governed by binary or digital codes (with Mondrian as the paradigm case), and from the temptation to allow the diagram as such to take over, which produces the opposite descent into a purely manual space (with Pollock as the paradigm case). Bacon's path—which should obviously be seen not in terms of any aesthetic or artistic superiority, but simply as his own path, where he discovers a "logic of sensation" peculiar to his work: Deleuze always stresses that great artists are incomparable—is to preserve and enhance the tension between form and disfiguration, instead of transcending it in either direction.

This, Deleuze suggests, is why Bacon and those that follow his path focus on color, as an intensity that acts directly on the nervous system. It is also why line and drawing in a particular and restricted sense, i.e., as <u>disegno</u> opposed to <u>colore</u> within the system set up by the Renaissance theorists, can be understood is secondary to color as intensity, and the reason for Deleuze's emphasis on the primacy of the haptic over the optical. This distinction, with roots in Alois Riegl and Wilhelm Worringer, is however here given a new twist that eventually overcomes the division between the terms. The haptic is all about proximity, the fusion of painter, object, and spectator in

7. A further and final encounter would be located at the level of the necessary **return** from such an Outside, where a relative and precarious interiority must be constituted, if death and dispersal is not to have the final word. In Deleuze and Foucault, but to a certain extent also in Heidegger, this return is made through the figure of the **fold**, although each of them determines this in a different way. For a discussion of the idea of folding in this respect, see my **Essays, Lectures** (Stockholm: Axl Books, 2007), 150ff.

8. The reading of Bacon is in fact one of the places where Deleuze engages in one of his most productive debates with phenomenology, although it is only rarely named in the text. For a discussion, see **Deleuze et la phénoménologie** (Mons: Les Editions Sils Maria, 2004), 160-169.

9. The idea of the "figural" is derived from JEAN-FRANÇOIS LYOTARD'S early work **Discours, figure** (Paris: Klincksieck, 1971), where Lyotard attempts to combine, but finally also transgress, phenomenology and psychoanalysis. Lyotard would later abandon these theories, and their potential for articulating a theory of the visual arts has remained strangely uncharted. Together with Daniel Birnbaum I hope to be able to explore these issues further in a coming book; a brief sketch of the argument can be found in our essay "Thinking Philosophy, Spatially: Jean-François Lyotard's 'Les Immatériaux' and the Philosophy of the Exhibition," in J. Backstein, D. Birnbaum, and S.-O. Wallenstein (eds.): **Thinking Worlds: The Moscow Conference on Philosophy, Politics, and Art** (New York and Berlin: Sternberg Press, 2008).

10. **Francis Bacon: Logique de la sensation** (Paris: Éditions de la Différence, 1981), 65. Bacon himself refers to his fascination with the texture of rhinoceros skin in the interviews with Sylvester. The idea of "Sahara" is also the organizing idea in one of the best monographs on Deleuze's aesthetics, MIREILLE BUYDENS, **Sahara: L'esthétique de Gilles Deleuze** (Paris: Vrin, 1990).

an "aformal" element—which for Deleuze must be distinguished from the "informal" in postwar French abstraction (to which much of his rhetoric may seem close, at least if viewed from a more "normal" art-critical perspective)—that introduces a Sahara of continual variations: to paint Sahara, nothing but Sahara, even in a single apple... The optical would on the other hand entail the emphasis on the distance in figure-ground relations, the introduction of narrative content and a whole space of representation. But if opticality traditionally asserts a priority of the line, then Deleuze, drawing freely on Worringer's <u>Abstraktion und Einfühlung</u>, finally discovers another type of line that no longer connects pre-existing points in a system of coordinates, but becomes a nomadic force that generates the points rather then joining them within an already given grid (which is one of the ways in which Deleuze describes the difference between a "smooth" and a "striated" space, in the vocabulary he borrows from Pierre Boulez). An instance of this he also finds in Klee, whose <u>Schöpferische Konfession</u> contains the famous phrase that Deleuze cites on many occasions, and which here too guides the aesthetic of force developed in the particular reading of Bacon: "art does not render the visible, art renders visible" ("Kunst gibt nicht das Sichtbare wieder, sondern macht sichtbar").[11] The eye and the hand, the optical and the manual, are then finally superseded in a third element, to which Deleuze points in the concluding paragraph, where he speaks of "the formation of a third eye, a haptic eye, a haptic vision of the eye, a new type of clarity. It is as if the duality between the tactile and the optical had been visually transcended in the direction of a haptic function that emerges from the diagram."[12] Color and line can finally not be opposed, since they are part of one and the same event, one and the same logic of sensation.

If the Foucauldian diagram has to do with the formation of archives of knowledge, and as it were constitutes the differential element of force into which practices and discourses are located, but also points in the direction of an act of thought, a "Fiat" that exceeds both knowledge and action, the Baconian diagram can perhaps be taken as a particular version, a local practice, whose condition of possibility however resides in the general, "aformal" dimension in which it always plunges.

And finally, if we were to lead both of these versions of the diagram back to their common root, we should go back to the most general presentation of the term in <u>A Thousand Plateaus</u>. In the fifth plateau, "587 B.C.—A.D. 70: On Several Regimes of Signs," it appears to be a particular aspect of the "abstract machine," and here we get a series of definitions, the most succinct of which is perhaps that the diagram is that which has "neither substance nor form, neither content nor expression," and "retains the most deterritorialized content and the most deterritorialized expression, in order to conjugate them."[13] Understood in this way, this diagrammatic and/or abstract machine "does not function to represent, even something real, but rather constructs a real that is yet to come, a new type of reality. Thus when it constitutes points of creation or potentiality it does not stand outside history but is instead always 'prior to' history. Everything escapes, everything creates — never alone, but through an abstract machine that produces continuums of intensity, effects conjunctions of deterritorialization, and extracts expressions and contents" (p. 157). But in traversing the different "plateaus," we also encounter many other instances of diagrams, related but surely not identical: the "short-term memory" of the "rhizome or diagram type" opposed to a "long-term memory" that is "arborescent and centralized" (p. 17); the abstract machine which "cuts across all stratifications, develops alone and in its own right on the plane of consistency whose diagram it constitutes" (p. 62); a Foucauldian use which inverts the terms, and defines the diagram as "a single abstract machine for the prison and the school and the barracks and the hospital and the factory" (p. 74); "the abstract Machine, or abstract Machines, insofar as they construct that body [without organs] or draw that plane or "diagram" what occurs (lines of flight, or absolute deterritorializations)"; a "true abstract machine [that] pertains to an assemblage in its entirety" and which is "defined as the diagram of that assemblage" (p. 101; cf. 110f); a diagram that is opposed to a stratified semiotics, although "even an asignifying diagram harbors knots of coincidence just waiting to form virtual centers of signifiance and points of subjectification" (p. 153); the list could go on. A close analysis of the minute shifts in terminology throughout the book, or any precise distinction between diagram and machine, would however probably lead us astray and simply create a kind of pseudo-clarity: the terminologies of Deleuze (and Guattari) remain in constant flux where old terms are picked up in new constellations in which their significance is enriched, and what we should attempt to catch is rather something like a tension or a movement toward a certain experience of thought, and not a precise definition that would immobilize the movement.

11.   Cf. PAUL KLEE, "Schöpferische Konfession", in **Schriften. Rezensionen und Aufsätze** (Cologne: Dumont Verlag 1976), 118-122. On the idea of line in Klee, cf. Deleuze, **The Fold**, trans. Tom Conley (Minneapolis: University of Minnesota Press, 1993), chap. 2.

12.   Logique de la sensation, 103.

13.   A Thousand Plateaus: Capitalism and Schizophrenia, trans. Brian Massumi (Minneapolis: University of Minnesota Press, 1987), 156. The following quotes from this book are given with page reference in the text.

14. This too is of course one of the great themes of DELEUZE and GUATTA-RI'S work, from the 1975 book on Kafka, through **A Thousand Plateaus** and onwards. For a discussion on segments vs. lines of flight, cf. in particular plateau 9, "Micropolitics and segmentarity." I have attempted to develop this theme in relation Fahlström's idea of games in "Every Way in is a Way out," together with Erik van der Heeg, in **Öyvind Fahlström**, exh. cat. (Valencia: IVAM Centre Julio Gonzalez, 1992).

15. Here I draw on a manuscript by the artist, forthcoming in **Atlantique** in spring 2009. Many works and reflections that address these issues can be found in NEIDICH'S earlier book **Blow-Up: Photography, Cinema and the Brain** (New York: DAP, 2003). DELEUZE AND GUATTARI develops the idea of "noology" particularly in **What is philosophy?**, but the theme is announced already in works from the late 1960s, for instance **The Logic of Sense and Difference and Repetition**. For MAURIZIO LAZZARATO'S idea of "noology" as a "second **bios**" relating to the brain, cf. for instance **La politica dell'evento** (Cosenza: Rubbittino, 2004), and **Les Révolutions du capitalisme** (Paris: Empêcheurs de penser en rond, 2004). For a discussion of these themes, as they have been developed by Lazzarato, Paolo Virno, and a whole series of thinkers and activists in the Italian "post-workerist" (**postoperaista**) movement, see the translations and introductory essays in **SubStance**, #112. Vol. 36, no. 1, 2007. For a discussion of the related idea of "autonomy" in relation to Italian architectural debates, see PIER VITTORIO AURELI, **The Project of Autonomy, The: Politics and Architecture Within and Against Capitalism** (New York: Princeton Architectural Press, 2008)

III

How can we make use of this manifold of possible diagrams, which in itself seems to be diagrammed, or traversed by a kind of diagrammatic movement? Warren Neidich's drawings, multicolored abstract schemas containing large subsections connected by multiple passages and sometimes minute connections, have gone through various stages, from the physical to the immaterial. As an ongoing mapping of our cultural condition, they are necessarily interminable, and even called upon to exist in terms of various supports and framing. Connecting continents with names like the Cultured Brain, the Global Generator, the Becoming Brain Drawing, and finally the Earthling Drawing, they resuscitate some of the humor of the variously named parts in Duchamp's <u>Large Glass</u>, but perhaps even more the infernal logic of Öyvind Fahlström's attempts from the later period of his work to produce flow-charts, for instance in the form of Monopoly games, which would map the world of capital and politics. The world system is both a paranoid machine revolving around the law of a Symbolic order (the flag, the nation, the president, the phallus, the great Signifier...) that constantly reproduces binary forms, closed segments, discontinuous architectural and organizational fragments, as well as a schizoid undoing of the machine—the other side of the diagram, which makes all the segments resonate, opens transversal communications, and shows us that a system is defined more by its leakages and lines of flights than by its hard and "segmented" order.[14]

The diagram has its pedagogical dimensions, it is an index or a "showing," which is why the act of pointing, the in-dexical movement, is an integral part of the artist's strategy to lead us into the diagram. From a random point of departure—all introductions to the labyrinth are of equal value, just as every exit is an entrance and every entrance an exit—we are lead onwards into an encyclopedia, which takes us from the "extensive" to the "intensive," from a space that contains the world, to ideas of the world, to techniques for altering both of them, and finally to modes of resistance to such transformations.

Much of Neidich's work takes its departure from the idea of "noology" and "noo-politics," as this has been developed by for instance Maurizio Lazzarato, but he extends and radicalizes it into his own idea of "neuropower."[15] Moving from the theory of cognitive capitalism to neuropower, Neidich invites us to reflect on the way in which images, brands, and various visual technologies impact directly on our brain, bypassing the censorships and reflective mechanisms of consciousness, but also on what kind of "image of thought" that this makes possible, not just as a passive causal effect, but as an active and constructive response. In a wider context, the visual arts, architecture, advertising, and media in general can be seen as part of the same process, whereby our minds are "sculpted" in order attain new levels of action and reaction. The neural interface—and we should remember that the science of neurology is precisely contemporary with cinema, which is surely not coincidental: the most powerful image technology for the re-visioning of the outer world is intertwined with the tool for investigating the substructure of our inner mental space—has become a site of conflict, even of political struggle, at a level which extends below that of human subjectivity and integrates consciousness in a process of transformation which is neither nature nor culture. Neuropower, as Neidich understands it, would inscribe itself on the most fundamental level of mental life, where our most basic affects and ideas are organized, where memory, fantasy, and intelligence emerge, and where a certain "neural plasticity" is at work.[16]

To such a process one might react differently—from the rejection that any artistic engagement in a domain such as "neural plasticity" no doubt provokes within a traditional humanist culture, to the complete immersion one encounters in the contemporary neo-Futurist techno-culture. Warren Neidich's way into this universe seems to be a kind of reflective fascination, combining both a theoretical desire to conceptualize and a profound physical attraction. For better or worse, we are inside a violent mutation of our sensorium, and there is no way back to a theory of subjectivity and experience that would remain untouched by it.

The question that his work poses is a crucial one: what position do the visual arts occupy, indeed what position can they at all occupy, in this vast transformation, which concerns not only images as we normally apprehend them through media or in institutionalized spaces of art, but in fact extend into the sphere of what used to be called the unconscious, the articulation of life and consciousness on a pre-subjective level, and even into the basic biological features of living beings? Should art and artists attempt to provide pockets of resistance, residual modes of experience that yet remain to be colonized by technology; should they inversely intensify these processes, perhaps in the sense of the "nihilism" earlier encountered by Nietzsche, and show us that the death of the supersensuous world opens up a world of perspectivism ruled neither by God nor Man, but by chance and necessity; or must they be content with simply recording and reflecting on a process whose determining factors are located elsewhere, in the flows of Capital itself, which then would appear as the successor of God and Nature, as the great Other to which we all must subject, both in the sense of mere subjection and the active response of becoming-subject?

The option suggested by Warren Neidich's work seems to be that there must be some other way to enter into this process—or better, since we are ineluctably part of it, to inhabit it, with body and mind alike—to steer it into the direction of a possible General Intelligence. Here he draws on ideas that have been developed by Paolo Virno in his analysis of post-Fordist labor as subjectivity and the development of a new "virtuosity."[17] The idea of inhabiting, although doing so in a more thoughtful and reflective way, perhaps indicates that the model of resistance and dialectical negation is no longer directly useful here (although I think it would be premature to simply abandon it). Since late modernist theory, the capacity of the work of art to open up a space of freedom has predominantly been understood in terms of its interiorization of the formal contradictions of society, whereby it would create a reflective distance towards the real. Today, the rethinking of critical theory that has been underway at least since the 1970s and posthumous publications of Adorno's Aesthetic Theory, to some seems to necessitate a dismantling of the very idea of resistance and the critical, which in many cases (for instance, in the ideas of the "postcritical," the "operative," and the "instrumental" in recent architectural discourse) appears to border on sheer acquiescence and subjection to the forces that be, although dressed up in a vocabulary of networks and intelligent production. Beyond such alternatives, the proposal of these diagrammatic drawings, as well as of those diverse theoretical models that they engage, must be understood in terms of a mutation into some other stance, based neither on rejection or affirmation, but on the possibility to release a different potential inside the forces of Capital.

Warren Neidich's diagrams insert themselves in this complex and still highly indeterminate mutation of Capital and its concomitant modes of perception, experience, and action in an active fashion, and their suggestion seems to be a demand that we should not only think more intensely and question our own propositions, and that we should not be afraid to discard inherited ideas of what constitutes mind, subjectivity, and experience, even the "human" as such, but that this rethinking as such is already an act of resistance, albeit in a new way, and that it invites us to conceive of artistic work as a tool for thinking that goes beyond the institutional framework of art and artist alike. The "redistribution of the sensible," of which Jacques Rancière speaks, and to which Neidich refers in several of his texts, must in this perspective be understood as transcending the sphere of art as well as politics, since it eventually affects the very fabric of life, the underlying substructures of the mind. The political challenges of such a redistribution are of course formidable: how should we conceive of an ethics or a politics, how should we account for the formation of a possible ethical or political agency, when the "multitude" that it must organize and integrate—without reducing it into the all-too classical form of a subject, individual or collective—extends beyond what we normally circumscribe by the use of our inherited humanist categories?

In asking such questions, and doing so within a horizon of certain optimism, Warren Neidich shares the utopian convictions of many of today's radical political thinkers, which call upon the "virtuosity" inherent in "immaterial labor," or the potentials that are set free by the advent of "Cognitive Capitalism." Whether this is a radical shift, or a mirage produced by the inexorable logic of Capital itself, as many of those who uphold the ethos of the traditional Left have argued, remains to be seen. Suffice it to say that whatever it is that is happening to us, it releases a certain transformative energy that needs to be cultivated, and that plunging into chaos may be a risk that we may need to take.

Warren Neidich's diagrammatic drawings are schemas for thinking, ways of connecting parts of our culture and history which for those entrenched in the average curricula of academic thought appear as hermetically sealed off from each other. Charting new and even non-existent territories—for to think, write, and create, as Deleuze and Guattari say, has to do with mapping and measuring territories, and above all those that do not yet exist—they incite us to trace new connections, although without providing any definite answer to what the outcome will be. The artist points his finger and leads us into the diagram; it is up to us to perform the rest.

16. Here too there is decisive inspiration from the work of Deleuze, particularly the two books on movement and time in cinema. Cinema, Deleuze argues, does not accommodate itself to pre-conceived theories of perception and synthesis, such as phenomenology and psychoanalysis, it traces and establishes new connections in the brain itself, and this is why it always has a close connection to philosophy. In producing new space-times, cinema forces us to once more ask Heidegger's question "what is called thinking/what calls upon us to think?" ("Was heisst Denken?"), not as a resistance to technology, or even as an attempt to think the "unthought essence" of technology, but as a way to intensify the possibility of expanding thought on the basis of the most recent image technologies, which obviously have developed a long way since Deleuze's two books were first published in 1983 and 1985. For a recent discussion of image, time, and perception in relation to post-Fordist capitalism, see also MAURIZIO LAZZARATO, **Videofilosofia. La percezione del tempo nel postfordismo** (Rome: Manifesto Libri, 1997).

17. See for instance his **A Grammar of the Multitude** (Los Angeles: Semiotext(e), 2004).

13

Neuropower Up   Lia Gangitano

1. Introduction

Warren Neidich's work as an artist, writer, educator, and theorist explores the potential of Neuroaesthetics, a field he began to formulate in the mid-1990s, as a paradigm capable of describing the complex conditions of the 'now'—a moment in which global technological networks and novel potentialities for subjectivity are coming into greater focus and correlation to each other. As knowledge becomes ever more commodified, and labor increasingly immaterial, our notions of art, work, and politics call for a 'redistribution of the sensible.' Theorist Jacques Rancière described 'the distribution of the sensible' as "...the system of division and boundaries that define, among other things, what is visible and audible within a particular aesthetico-political regime."[1] However, the condition of 'immaterial labor' itself (work as potential, not yet objectified, constituting labor as subjectivity) insinuates a high level of mutability, adaptability, and contingency that characterizes current cultural production, giving rise to new forms of intellectual coherence.

Neidich's decades-long project seeks to discern these simultaneous transformations, occurring in a seemingly endless and indiscernible feedback loop state, which impact both the cultural, social, and political realms and the networks of the brain, due to our distinctive neural plasticity. He has noted: "...the combination of new social definitions, the disembodied kinesthetic logics they engender, and the response in the fields of artistic and architectural production, for example, of 'trying to keep up' with these new compulsions brought about by revolutionary technologies, redefine our cultural context and call out to the brain's inherent dynamic architecture."[2] Historically, Neidich cites the transition that occurred at the turn of the last century as one of analog (extensive) to digital (intensive) culture, but also, taking cues from Fredric Jameson's Postmodernism, or, The Cultural Logic of Late Capitalism, acknowledges that the subject formed by "the space of high modernism" lagged a bit behind, and did not previously possess the "perceptual equipment to match this new hyperspace," imagined long before its current full-blown actualization.[3] It seems a new equivalence is at hand, and the 'now' is about 'becoming.'

2. Power Up

Power Up is a phrase I first heard when Julie Ault, founding member of the New York art collective Group Material (1979–1996), organized an exhibition for the Wadsworth Atheneaum in Hartford, CT, entitled Power Up: Sister Corita and Donald Moffett, Interlocking (1997). This was the first time I became consciously aware of Corita's work (which I had often seen in the form of public works—a painting on a natural gas tank along the Southeast Expressway in Dorchester, MA, and her 1985 Love stamp for the US postal service). This pairing of two artists separated by generation but joined by their integration of popular culture, graphics, and art for the purpose of addressing social change, highlights the cultural affinities of the 60s and 90s, perhaps illuminating the critical junctures that preceded, and at which we arrived, roughly following each of these decades. Corita's use of the words "Power Up" in a 1965 serigraph, like many of her pop graphic slogans, utilized the vernacular of the day to motivate political action (the phrase was borrowed from a gasoline ad and paired with text concerning hunger and class disparity by poet and peace activist Daniel Berrigan). Moffett's work as an artist, cofounder of the design firm Bureau, and member of the collective Gran Fury, utilized various advertising strategies to bring messages concerning HIV/AIDS to large-scale public audiences. Although aesthetically different, both Corita and Moffett used the apparatuses, materials, and production skills of their day to reach audiences defined by specific perceptual habits, to instruct and disclose the conditions of power and their biopolitical import.

A borrowing between aesthetics and politics is perhaps characteristic of these two particular decades, the 60s and 90s. In observing movements that preceded each of them, it is interesting to note that certain prior developments also called for a more extensive engagement, reflected in the cultural realm. In this context, the field of culture can be understood as a viscous medium that supports political, social, economic, historical, and spiritual languages, and allows for a certain degree of interactivity. As such, these languages form an amalgam of shifting concepts and conditions in which we are immersed. The 60s

1.   GABRIEL ROCKHILL, "Translator's Introduction: Jacques Rancière's Politics of Perception," Jacques Rancière, **The Politics of Aesthetics, The Distribution of the Sensible**, (London: Continuum, 2004): 1.

2.   WARREN NEIDICH, "Neuropower," draft of essay to be published in **Atlantica** (forthcoming 2009).

3.   FREDRIC JAMESON, "Culture," **Postmodernism, or The Cultural Logic of Late Capitalism**, (Durham, North Carolina: Duke University Press, 1991): 38-39.

and 90s are reflective of preceding compositions, but display important shifts. Like the conditions of 'the image of thought,' to be discussed later, these shifts represent the projection of circumstances imagined by artists, for example, echoing the historical transition, which began in the late 19th century, from an 'extensive' culture with its linear, hierarchical characteristics, to a nonlinear, rhizomatic 'intensive' culture. This transition makes possible the elaboration of display tactics—the opportunity to imagine and create slogans and iconography representative of this new space.

Looking at the micropolitical events that shaped the characteristics of many waves of Modernism (Constructivism, Impressionism, Cubism, Abstract Expressionism, Pop Art, etc.) mitigates their repetition as eternal return (in which Color Field painting, for example, simulates early Constructivist painting) and instead suggests the actions of the avant-garde are instituted upon the nature of subjectivity itself. In his discussion of postwar American and Latin American art of the 1950s, art historian Benjamin Buchloh explains: "These practices appear no longer to originate in the cultural matrix of the nation-state, or in the fictions of national identity as their ultimate social anchoring ground. [...] Their 'international style,' by contrast, seems to have shifted (perhaps already starting with Abstract Expressionism) toward a model of cultural production that is ultimately grounded in the economic structures of advanced global corporate capitalism that have definitively left those conditions of traditional identity formation behind."[4] Neidich elaborates that the conditions and contextual frameworks of the classic avant-garde and that of the neo-avant-garde are entirely different, making primary and secondary iterations unique. In his words, there is no reason to account for the eternal return as degenerate. His project as a whole points to the fact that this is not only a cultural and philosophical argument, but a neurobiological one as well.

"The avant-garde can never be understood in terms of reductive, empirical material paradigms because the nature of the avant-garde itself is always about the sublime conditions of the work of art, which are always beyond the recognition facilities the perceiving subject has on hand. As such, the avant-garde is essentially a future-oriented paradigm of what is not obvious in the deep substrate of meaning, what is 'yet to become' in the vast milieu of

significance. Culture as it was in its social dreams, and as it will be in its future prognostication, constantly unwraps the possibilities that lay inherent in the history of the species itself, collaged as it is upon the matrix of evolving memory as it is positioned in artworks, buildings, urban and virtual spaces."[5]

While acknowledging the seemingly forward-looking nature of prior aesthetic movements (for example, abstraction in the 50s), an engagement with overt political realities was similarly absent in the 50s and in postmodernism of the 80s. For once again, in looking slightly backward and slightly forward, postmodern theory, in an attempt to level such categories as aesthetics and politics altogether, also may have missed the point. As Neidich has noted: "Perhaps the initial reception of [...] avant-garde excess proclaims a misrecognition; [further] postmodernism's misunderstanding of this misrecognition, in its attempt to understand the work of art in an expanded cultural and social field, led to its demise as a condition of social change."[6]

In his 1982 lecture, "Postmodernism and Consumer Society," Fredric Jameson defined postmodernism as a "periodizing concept" that is characterized by "the erosion of the older distinction between high culture and so-called mass or popular culture," and "whose function is to correlate the emergence of new formal features in culture with the emergence of a new type of social life and a new economic order—what is often euphemistically called modernization, postindustrial or consumer society, the society of the media or the spectacle, or multinational capitalism."[7] In addition to the rejection of prior modernist values and forms that sought to embody truth, originality, and universality, he goes on to outline key features of postmodernism such as pastiche, mimicry, schizophrenia, and their reflection of a fragmented sense of space and time, characteristic of the postmodern moment. Doubt is cast, as well, in Jameson's figuration of the individual postmodern subject: "[I]n the classic age of competitive capitalism, in the heyday of the nuclear family and the emergence of the bourgeoisie as the hegemonic social class, there was such a thing as individualism, as individual subjects. But today, in the age of corporate capitalism, [...] of bureaucracies in business as well as in the state, [...] that older bourgeois individual subject no longer exists." He notes a poststructuralist position would add, "...not only is the bourgeois individual subject a thing of the past, it is also

4.   BENJAMIN H. D. BUCHLOH, **Neo-Avantgarde and Culture Industry; Essays on European and American Art from 1955-1975**, (Cambridge, MA and London: October Books, MIT Press): xx.

5.   WARREN NEIDICH, correspondence with the author, January 2009.

6.   WARREN NEIDICH, **"Political Art of the Sixties was About Delineation, Political Art today is About Delineation,"** artist's description, 2008.

7.   FREDRIC JAMESON, "Postmodernism and Consumer Society," **The Anti-Aesthetic: Essays on Postmodern Culture,** ed. Hal Foster (Seattle: Bay Press, 1983): 112-113.

a myth; it <u>never</u> really existed in the first place; there have never been autonomous subjects of that type."[8]

Jean-François Lyotard in his essay "What Is Postmodernism?" argues that postmodernism is merely and already "a part of the modern," caught in a dialectical process whereby "...in an amazing acceleration, the generations precipitate themselves."[9] This conflation is perhaps aptly demonstrated in the contradictory conservatism of the art world of the 1980s, characterized by an increasing over-valuation of media attention and the aggrandizement of wealth, which precipitated an elitism that postmodernism (and Pop Art before it) initially sought to remedy. Jameson ended his landmark lecture with a question: "We have seen that there is a way in which postmodernism replicates and reproduces—reinforces—the logic of consumer capitalism; the more significant question is whether there is also a way in which it resists that logic." To this question, Neidich's work may propose: Neuropower Up.[10]

3. Political Art of the Sixties was About Delineation, Political Art Today is About Differentiation

One of Neidich's recent drawings, <u>Political Art of the Sixties was About Delineation, Political Art today is About Differentiation</u> (2008), originally existed as a drawing on paper, constituting the left margin of a larger wall drawing of the same name, initially installed at IASPIS Studio in Stockholm. The right margin was fitted with a white neon sign that read: "If it looks like art it probably isn't." Later, the drawing resurfaced in a projected installation at Onomatopee in Eindhoven under the rubric, <u>Lost Between the Extensivity/Intensivity Exchange</u>. Here, the larger handmade drawing was fragmented into a series of smaller drawings, photocopied on clear plastic, and distributed onto a number of overhead projectors dispersed throughout the space. Some of the drawings projected onto the walls of the space, others onto participants wearing white shirts, and some onto the white surfaces of pedestals borrowed from galleries and museums. Given the relative obsolescence of the equipment used (the overhead projector) and its institutional style, paired with the educational directness of a diagrammatic method of drawing, this immaterial mapping spelled out a complex historical transition. On the one hand, its initial inspiration was the psychogeographic mappings of the Situationists, and on the other, "the dynamic qualities of the signals of the brain during thinking, like a mental

map, in which the present is recategorized in relationship to multiple memory maps distributed throughout the brain."[11] Further, this combination of equipment and image elicited the relative speed with which we shift from past to present, also reminding the viewer that this knowledge is cumulative, as the past is not replaced or obliterated, but rather becomes folded into an understanding of the present.

<u>Political Art of the Sixties...</u> seeks to outline the implicit power relations that surrounded artistic production in the 60s, against which practitioners of conceptual art and institutional critique, for example, sought to delineate their work, as if they could somehow operate from outside this sphere of relations. However, as Andrea Fraser has recently noted, "Moving from a substantive understanding of 'the institution' as specific places, organizations, and individuals to a conception of it as a social field, the question of what is inside and what is outside becomes much more complex."[12] This question of inside/outside has consistently beleaguered modernism, because it is undermined by the very dialectic of extensivity/intensivity prompted by modernist thought. Dan Graham, in his "My Works for Magazine Pages: 'A History of Conceptual Art'," cites his early experience, in the mid-60s, as manager of the John Daniels Gallery in midtown New York, and his exposure to a group of artists, including Sol Lewitt, Donald Judd, and Robert Smithson, but particularly Dan Flavin, as instigation for his subsequent interest in "the possibility of dematerialized, noncommodified art forms and a more politically engaged role for the artist."[13] He noted: "The fall after the gallery failed, I began experimenting with art works that could be read as a reaction against the gallery experience, but also as a response to contradictions I discerned among gallery artists. While American Pop Art of the early 1960s referred to the surrounding media world of cultural information as a framework, Minimalist art works of the mid-to-late 1960s seemed to refer to the gallery interior cube as the ultimate contextual frame of reference or support for the work."[14]

However, these frameworks could not long maintain the structural transparency necessary to distinguish critical artworks within an economy that consistently sought to assimilate them, giving them value within the very structures they sought to critique. Perhaps due to the fact that Graham "...seems to have acknowledged that their original radicality in questioning the role of the artwork in its social context had been given up

8.   JAMESON: 115.

9.   JEAN-FRANÇOIS LYOTARD, "What Is Postmodernism?" **Art and Its Significance: An Anthology of Aesthetic Theory**, ed. Stephen David Ross, (Albany: State University of New York Press, 1994): 561-64.

10. JAMESON, "Postmodernism and Consumer Society": 125.

11. WARREN NEIDICH, email correspondence with the author, 2008.

12. ANDREA FRASER, "From the Critique of Institutions to an Institution of Critique," **Artforum**, September 2005: 281.

13. BRIAN WALLIS, "Dan Graham's History Lessons," **Rock My Religion 1965-1990**, eds. Brian Wallis and Dan Graham, (Cambridge, Massachusetts: The MIT Press, 1994): viii.

14. DAN GRAHAM, "My Works for Magazine Pages: 'A History of Conceptual Art'," **Rock My Religion 1965-1990**: xviii.

and that minimal works had been restored easily into the commodity status acquiring exchange value inasmuch as they gave up their context-bound idea of use value…"[15] he instead adopted a form that made "no claim for itself as 'Art'," selecting the "informational frame" of the magazine.[16] But information itself is the currency of intensive culture. Intensive culture is characterized by nonequivalence and difference. Whereas extensive culture produces the commodity as a form of equivalence, intensive culture is described best by the idea of the brand: "Products no longer circulate as identical objects, already fixed, static and discrete, determined by the intentions of their producers. Instead, cultural entities spin out of the control of their makers: in their circulation they move and change through transposition and translation, transformation and transmogrification. […] In global culture industry, products move as much through accident as through design, as much by virtue of their unintended consequences as through planned design or intention."[17]

Following in a long tradition that spans the disciplines of art, architecture, philosophy, linguistics, and science, Neidich has chosen the intensive logics of the diagram, a format laden as much with information as it is with shape, color, and line, to aid in the production of ideas. Like the pages of a journal, Neidich's drawings, mappings, and diagrams resist easy categorization within a given field, and can recall a range of references from Jacques Lacan's "Schema L" (1955) to Warhol's "Dance Diagram" (1962). Deploying this format toward future-oriented action reflective of the current cultural moment, Neidich points out in Political Art Today… "[art] must address the homogenizing effect on culture of Neo-liberal Global Capitalism, which through the creative industries, art market, branding, and advertising has created a crisis in the production of difference and variation. Art must resist this homogenizing condition. […] Art is a condition of the future and must await parallel and commensurate changes in the social, psychological, spiritual, economic, and historical fabric before it can obtain full meaning."[18]

4. Diagram as Thread or, Conceptual Art as Neurobiological Praxis and its Antecedents

My engagement with Neidich's project began around 1997, as a newly appointed curator at Thread Waxing Space, New York. In taking this job, I inherited a rather large box of unsolicited exhibition proposals to

review. Known for exhibition projects that favored curatorial experimentation in an alternative, large-scale context, Thread Waxing Space's stash of proposals read like an archive of reiterations of what had come to be considered "pathetic art," a term made distinct by curator Ralph Rugoff in the early 90s. As art critic Irving Sandler noted:

"Art of the end of the 1980s took three diverse directions. The first extended available twentieth-century styles in personal ways, disregarding social issues. The second—which commanded the most art-world attention—dealt directly with newly urgent social problems, and the third was aptly labeled abject or pathetic art. […] Ralph Rugoff wrote, […] 'Bereft of irony's protective distance, pathetic art invites you to identify with the artist as someone [not] in control of his or her culture…. […] Pathetic art knows it doesn't have the strength; its position of articulation is already disabled and impaired….' Rugoff concluded that pathetic art was a reflection of a society and a culture that were dysfunctional and out-of-gas and whose future did not seem to offer any improvement."[19]

Perhaps it was its optimism, or the marked difference between the strains of pathetic art and the sense of intellectual agency attributed by Neidich to artists and works, that drew me to his weirdly uncomplicated proposal, entitled Conceptual Art as Neurobiological Praxis. It also could have been the visual material included—not necessarily that of the artists in the exhibition—but diagrams roughly drawn by Neidich, illustrating neologisms drawn from concepts of neurobiology as they might correspond with historical and contemporary art. The exhibition was divided into three parts, according to the diagram: the Retinal-Cortical Axis (visual processing); the Word-Image Dialectic; and Global Chaosmosis (a term invented by Neidich referring to the operations of the entire brain, derived from both Gilles Deleuze's notions of chaosmosis and the rhizome, and Gerald Edelman and Jean-Pierre Changeux's 'global mapping' in relation to the development of the brain as it is shaped by experience). This category is the foundation of Neidich's more recent arguments concerning the ways in which intensive culture sculpts the brain.

The diagrams and proposal posited that conceptual art was/is not "a linear prac-

CONCEPTUAL ART AS NEUROBIOLOGICAL PRAXIS, 1999, installation view, Thread Waxing Space, New York City.

15.   B.H.D. BUCHLOH, "Moments of History in the work of Dan Graham," **Dan Graham Articles**, (Eindhoven: Van Abbemuseum, 1978): 75.

16. Dan Graham cited in BUCHLOH: 73.

17.   SCOTT LASH AND CELIA LURY, "Introduction: Theory-Some Signposts," **Global Culture Industry: The Mediation of Things**, (Cambridge: Polity Press, 2007): 4-5.

18. NEIDICH, **"Political Art of the Sixties was About Delineation, Political Art today is About Differentiation."**

19. IRVING SANDLER, "Into the 1990s," **Art of the Postmodern Era: From the Late 1960s to the Early 1990s**, (Westview Press, 1996): 547-548.

APPARATUS,
1998, video still

20. WARREN NEIDICH, "Conceptual Art
as Neurobiological Praxis,"
**The Alternative to What? Thread Waxing Space
and the 90s**, (Foundation 20 21 and
Participant Inc, forthcoming).

21. NEIDICH, "Conceptual Art as
Neurobiological Praxis."

22. NEIDICH, email correspondence with
the author, 2008.

23. CEDRIC PRICE, Architect (1934-
2003), Design Museum, London,
website, designmuseum.org.

24. JEAN-LOUIS VIOLEAU quoting JEAN
BAUDRILLARD in, "Utopie: In Acts,"
**The Inflatable Moment: Pneumatics and Protest
in '68** (Princeton Architectural Press
and the Architectural League of
New York, 1999): 53.

tice [but instead] emerges in the context of many streams of art practice including Lettrism and Situationism; philosophy including Structuralism and Phenomenology; Infomatics like Cybernetics; psychological discourses like psychoanalysis; as well as Marxism and political activism of the late 60s."[20] In retrospect, Conceptual Art as Neurobiological Praxis seems to envision the advance of prior iterations of immaterial labor, including conceptual art, as inseparable from current understandings of art and its relationship to popular culture, media, politics—and the significance, for new generations of artists, of historical predecessors who imagined this hybrid state. As Neidich noted in relation to the exhibition project:

> "For it is within this complexity [of folded structures] that other forms and other meanings hibernate, latent, remaining in a state of hypothermia and very slow metabolism, waiting for the proper set of conditions in which to emerge and once again 'become,' only slightly changed, especially in regard to interpretation. [...] Some would argue that an explanation of this phenomena can be found in the way that the social, political, historical, psychological, economic conditions of the late 90s and early 21st century share important qualities with those of the late 60s and early 70s, such that certain works [which have gained renewed interest] express key insights common to both eras."[21]

5. From Hybrid Dialectic to Dynamic Collage

Neidich has recently directed me to his videos as a fundamental framework for all his work, "slipping into the spaces between the lines as if they were an architectural edifice by Cedric Price,"[22] an architect driven by the goal of nurturing change. His goal was "enabling people to think the unthinkable. Through projects, drawings, and teaching, Price (1934-2003) overturned the notion of what architecture is by suggesting radical ideas of what it might be."[23] Coincidentally, at the time of our initial meeting, I was involved in an exhibition project concerning architecture of the 60s, Research Architecture: Selections from the FRAC Orleans Collection (co-curated with Philippe Barriere and Bill Menking, organized by Thread Waxing Space in conjunction with Pratt Institute and the University of Kansas). The exhibition project was based on the premise that an

engagement with the imaginations of the past, during moments when technological advances render increasingly tangible the theoretical experiments of prior generations, is reflected in contemporary practices—another aspect of catching up with a future imagined in the past.

Research Architecture posited that against the repressive forces concretized in institutional architecture of the 60s, for example, futurisms of the past and the visionary authors who imagined them existed—with or without the actual technological means to realize their dreams. The availability of tools that enable the rendering of widespread hallucinatory spectacle, global communications, etc., across real space and time doesn't necessarily make them better, or more real, than the speculative projects of the 60s by Archigram, Utopie Group, Superstudio, or Buckminster Fuller. These artists and groups integrated themes from popular culture and politics within radical intellectual frameworks to expand the fields of art and architecture, mainly through works made of paper and cardboard, and unaided by computers.

These predominantly ephemeral histories of utopian art and architecture run parallel to the still-persistent inheritance of modern rationalist methodologies—outlining that there were other, less tangible, societal dreams at play. Not always explicitly oppositional (although hostage-taking did occur at conferences involving Utopie, Archigram, Superstudio, and Archizoom), these projects were oriented toward a different future than the one we typically experience today, and they achieved this alien status by challenging the accepted links between artistic forms and representation—seeking, instead, to demystify the objects of art and architecture.

> "Basically [Utopie] attempted to transcend architecture itself, as they transcended urban planning itself, like the Situationists could scrap the university milieu itself.... Everyone found himself at ground zero of the destruction of his own discipline. There was a kind of dissolution by excess on which everyone could agree. [...] Within the framework of Utopie—and that's what Utopie was, too—we were searching for an intellectual center of gravity from where we could branch out to all the other disciplines."[24]

The potential for catching up from lag

times, and the complex processes of recuperating from cyclical approaches toward perceived annihilation of prior understandings, are precisely what gave <u>Conceptual Art as Neurobiological Praxis</u> its unusual optimism. Rather than the failure or death of previous movements, Neidich's thesis pointed to the ways in which these repositories of knowledge and action fuel the present, as they are folded into any potential that art, architecture, etc. may still possess as productive forces. This potential, shared by a newly conceived 'multitude,' could be described as the neurobiological sublime: "The lack of register between new and old forms of spaces and the lack of computability of a mind adapted to the conditions of the architectural past produce a new form of the unconscious and uncanny."[25] In his discussion of the 'multitude,' philosopher Paolo Virno also addresses the 'uncanny' as a key element:

> "Thus, there is nothing more shared and more common, and in a certain sense more <u>public</u>, than the feeling of 'not feeling at home.' No one is less isolated than the person who feels the fearful pressure of the indefinite world. [...] '[N]ot feeling at home' is in fact a distinctive trait of the concept of the multitude, while the separation of the 'inside' and the 'outside' [...] is what earmarked the [...] idea of people. [...] The multitude [...] is united by the risk which derives from 'not feeling at home,' from being exposed omnilaterally to the world."[26]

Accelerated circumstances, a lack of register between old and new, and an uncanny sense of the obsolescence of the present (such as Walter Benjamin's arcades—already replaced by department stores) were, perhaps, all foreshadowed in the landmark essay, "The Work of Art in the Age of Mechanical Reproduction," in which new technological conditions of reproduction or "post-production" were received with optimism. For Benjamin, the mediums of photography and film promised a democratized, participatory audience, necessarily operating in "an immense and unexpected field of action."[27] The significance of cinema and early cinematic devices in Neidich's work has taken various forms, including his video investigations such as <u>Brainwash</u> (1999), in which audience and actor view the turning of a black and white striped drum. Neidich's interest in this instrument emanates from its twofold purpose, as both an early cinematic zoetrope and a diagnostic neurological tool. On one hand, it is a device used by artists to create another kind of reality, and on the other, it is a device used by doctors to document and diagnose conditions of the brain. The video presents these two functions, with their distinct histories—one presumably subjective and the other objective—as inseparable. He has noted in relation to this work: "The body is part of the world and that world is to a certain extent formed by new technologies. These new technologies, especially as they affect time and space, affect the production of subjectivity. [...] The drum represents the effect of a new sublime condition brought about by cinema in the early 20th century; a condition that is related to the perceptual and cognitive systems of time and space."[28] Marcel Duchamp, fascinated by the congruencies of art, cinema, technology and science, exemplifies the link between transgressive artistic gestures and the positivistic advance of technology, moving toward a reorientation of the conditions of knowledge. Neidich's work emphasizes, as well, that art can and does investigate areas most notably relegated to science, like perception, and arrives at radically alternative paradigms.

In his discussion of Gilles Deleuze's concepts of cinematic time, philosopher John Rajchman makes reference to Duchamp's cinema books as a means to introduce a "new psycho-mechanics, a new way of affecting our nervous systems. [...] At the heart of Deleuze's analysis of cinematic images and their dispositifs, we find the problem of a determination of a time no longer defined by succession (past, present, future); of a space no longer defined by simultaneity (distinct elements in closed or framed space); and of a permanence no longer based in eternity (instead given as form of a complex variation)."[29] By overlapping creative technologies with those of a scientific nature, Neidich proposed a new assemblage, which he refers to as 'hybrid dialectic,' a new strain of the history of thought based on a novel set of perceptual conditions. His video works <u>Apparatus</u> (1998) and <u>Memorial Day</u> (1998) are cases in point delivering a video image which is the result of this superimposition and as a result producing an image that hovers between these two formerly distinct conditions of knowledge. In <u>Kiss</u> (2000), <u>360 degrees</u> (2000), and <u>Taos Pueblo Looping</u> (2000) another strategy is used. All involve a small video camera attached to a cane designed for the visually impaired. In <u>360 degrees</u> Neidich traces the form of an old found car blind folded creating a sound

MEMORIAL DAY,
1998, video still

MEMORIAL DAY,
1998, video still

25.   NEIDICH, "Neuropower."

26. PAOLO VIRNO, "Beyond the coupling of the terms fear/anguish," **A Grammar of the Multitude**, (Los Angeles and New York: Semiotext[e], 2004): 34.

27. WALTER BENJAMIN, "The Work of Art in the Age of Mechanical Reproduction," **Illuminations**, ed. Hannah Arendt, trans. Harry Zohn (New York: Schocken Books, 1968): 236.

28. WARREN NEIDICH, **Brainwash**, project description, 1999.

29. JOHN RAJCHMAN, "Deleuze's Time or How the Cinematic Changes Our Idea of Art," **Art and the Moving Image, A Critical Reader**, ed. Tanya Leighton (Tate Publishing and Afterall, 2008): 310.

TAOS PUEBLO LOOPING,
2000, video still

EARTHLING:
NEWSWEEK, PARIS,
2004, video installation.

30.   WARREN NEIDICH, **Earthling**,
       project description, 2006.

31.   NEIDICH, **Earthling**.

32.   JAMESON: 125.

33.   NEIDICH, **Earthling**.

34.   RICHARD KEARNEY, "The Crisis
       of the Post-modern Image,"
       Modern French Philosophy, ed. A.
       Phillips-Griffiths (Cambridge:
       Cambridge University Press,
       1987): 120.

35.   GILLES DELEUZE, "The Diagram,"
       Francis Bacon: The Logic of Sensation
       (Minneapolis: University of Minnesota
       Press, 2003): 83.

work in the process. Sighted in <u>360</u> and <u>Taos Peublo Looping</u> he uses the combined instrument to trace natural and cultural outlines as if with a pencil. Neidich's investigation is based on infirmity and disability. He chooses medical instruments used to diagnose maladjusted perceptual systems in order to conduct artistic research in direct opposition to modernist requirements of perfect coordinates. Similarly, more recent works attempt to combine overlapping subjectivities, reminiscent of cinematic consciousness.

Neidich's <u>Earthling</u> series of photographs and videos of improvised performances by amateur actors taking place in cafes (2006) makes reference to the role of media (newspapers, magazines) in "producing new subjectivities in the context of evolving global identities."[30] After collecting an archive of images sampled from newsstands, café tables, etc., around the world for about a year, Neidich began to frequent cafes, asking strangers if they would perform in his work. When someone agreed, he or she was given a choice from the collection of magazines and newspapers Neidich carried with him. Each had an image of the face of a notable person and a headline. Neidich then measured the size of the participant's eye or the distance between the eyes, in order to match holes cut out of the magazine or newspaper image—aligning the optical axis of the actor with that of the image on the page. The actor then improvised a performance, looking from behind the newspaper or magazine as if it were a mask. The photographs and videos that resulted are called 'dynamic collages,' drawing attention to the fact that the inanimate newspaper was superimposed upon a living human being. Although sharing similar intentions with, for example, the political collages of John Heartfield or Hannah Hoch, Neidich's political images and videos look very different. Like Corita and Moffett previously mentioned, these artists have used similar methodologies to describe extremely different times.

The photographs and videos that comprise <u>Earthling</u>, like other serialized projects by Neidich, insinuate the connections between "the history of apparatus, the history of the images they create, the history of the 'thought image' which results, as a way of the mind making sense of the new landscape of images that make up visual culture. That history has become condensed in the new logics of global media in which the nation state has been replaced by global culture and the apparatus to administer those new conditions has changed as

well."[31] If postmodern thought rendered impossible any sense of progress or transgressive individual agency, signaling a form of 'apocalyptic pessimism' described in Jameson's conclusion as symptomatic of late capitalism, and thematized as a disappearance of history, perhaps it was best exemplified by the news: "One is tempted to say that the very function of the news media is to relegate such recent historical experiences as rapidly as possible into the past. The informational function of the media would thus be to help us forget, to serve as the very agents and mechanisms for our historical amnesia."[32]

In Neidich's once again somewhat optimistic figuration, the postmodern aesthetic of ahistoricism seems almost old-fashioned, and nothing is forgotten. If news images are the lens through which we understand the world and our place in it, amidst today's maelstrom of information—images streaming past us, disappearing as quickly as they appear—a major transformation must be occurring. With <u>Earthling</u>, Neidich expands upon the 'hybrid dialectic,' with "the objective dispositif of the newspaper now directly linked to the organic body mind in a collaged interface."[33]

> "By collapsing the historical dimensions of time—recollection of time past and projection of the future—into an empty play of euphoric instants, post-modernism runs the risk of eclipsing the potential of human experience for liberation. It risks cultivating the ecstasy of self-annihilation by precluding the possibility of self-expression. And it risks abandoning the emancipatory practice of imagining alternative horizons of existence (remembered or anticipated) by renouncing the legitimacy of narrative coherence or identity. [...] The danger stalking the postmodern labyrinth is <u>nothingness</u>. The empty tomb. The paralyzing fear that there is nothing <u>after</u> post-modernism."[34]

6. Neuropower
Perhaps it is in Neidich's diagrammatic drawings that novel possibilities for the subject most freely float. Outlining in-depth studies, new orders, rhizomatic processes, "the diagram is indeed a chaos, a catastrophe, but it is also a germ of order or rhythm."[35] It is here that branching histories and concepts of art, work, and politics play into mappings that suggest expansive po-

tentialities, tracing past intellectual actions with arrows pointing to a future. As Neidich notes: "This goes to the very heart of Neuro-power, as the site of control has now moved into the very brain centers that form our goal-directed habits and that influence the decisions we make before we even encounter the streaming conditions of the world that, in the end, we sample according to these internally generated conditions."[36]

In his forward to Paolo Virno's <u>A Grammar of the Multitude</u>, Sylvère Lotringer describes the important historical context from which the ideas of abstract intelligence and immaterial labor were born, in Italian 'worker-ism' (operaismo) or the Autonomia movement of the 70s. Linking labor, politics, and intellect, Autonomia sought, through researched activism, pirate radio, and direct actions, to develop alternative theories concerning the self-organization of labor. They articulated a diverse series of experiences based on a fundamental refusal of labor in the traditional sense. A sharp assessment of capitalist society, its powers, and its protagonists, Autonomia outlined new forms of communication and knowledge beyond the social relations dictated by waged labor. Based particularly on the conditions of factory workers, workerism maintained that workers' knowledge of the productive cycle resulted in the possibility to stop, to sabotage, to withdraw. Further, the absence of work becomes a time of communication, exchange, and social knowledge. Their theories grew away from the traditional Marxist notion of 'the people,' with its implication of a separation between inside/outside, and instead viewed the expanded field of social intelligence as the new labor force.

"The multitude is a new category in political thought. [...] It is, Virno suggests, open to plural experiences and searching for non-representative political forms, but 'calmly and realistically,' not from a marginal position. In a sense the multitude would finally fulfill Autonomia's motto—'the margins at the center'—through its active participation in socialized knowledge. [...] Everything has become 'performative.' Virno brilliantly develops here his major thesis, an analogy between virtuosity (art, work, speech) and politics. They all are political because they all need an audience, a publicly organized space, which Marx calls 'social co-operation,' and a common language in which to communicate. And they all are performance because they

find in themselves, and not in any end product, their own fulfillment."[37]

In Neidich's performative lecture, <u>Some cursory comments on the nature of my diagrammatic drawing</u>, (first presented in the studio at IASPIS in which his wall drawings were made in 2008), the artist is blindfolded. With the aid of an assistant, Neidich is spun around, but left facing one of the walls. Pointing, he walks toward the wall and lands on a word at random, which the assistant calls out. Turning toward the audience, Neidich then recites from memory all of the interwoven connections, definitions, and significations mapped out in the drawing for the duration of about one hour and a half. As Peggy Phelan has noted: "Performance's only life is in the present. Performance cannot be saved, recorded, documented, or otherwise participate in the circulation of representations of representations: once it does so, it becomes something other than performance. To the degree that performance attempts to enter the economy of reproduction it betrays and lessens the promise of its own ontology. Performance's being, like the ontology of subjectivity proposed here, becomes itself through disappearance."[38]

Much like Autonomia's notion of immaterial labor, Phelan's concept of performance as non-reproductive insinuates a new form of subjectivity, liberated from the "machinery of reproductive representation necessary to the circulation of capital. [...] Without a copy, live performance [...] disappears into memory, into the realm of invisibility and the unconscious where it eludes regulation and control."[39] Neidich's project takes these ideas into the area of Neuropower, which he defines as the means through which a constantly transforming cultural milieu sculpts the differences inherent in the nascent neurobiological potential of the brain, a process mostly occurring right after birth, but also continuing throughout life. "Neural Plasticity's potential as a field of differences can be molded according to the new conditions of post-Fordist deregulation, acting upon the conditions of the matter of the brain itself. I would like to suggest that this reconfiguration is actually the site of performative gestures, the non-reproductive labor of communicative virtuosos."[40]

Perhaps it is only when we move from the individual to the audience that these two theoretical frameworks, Phelan's concept of performance and Virno's notion of the virtuoso, merge. As a population of singularities, the audience of the multitude is a

EARTHLING: THE DAILY
TELEGRAPH, NEW YORK,
2005, Type-C print,
40 x 50in.

EARTHLING:
THE GUARDIAN, NEW YORK,
2005, Type-C print,
40 x 50in.

36. NEIDICH, **Neuropower**.

37. SYLVÈRE LOTRINGER, "Foreword: We, the Multitude," in Paolo Virno, **A Grammar of the Multitude** (Los Angeles and New York: Semiotext[e], 2004): 13.

38. PEGGY PHELAN, "The ontology of performance: representation without reproduction, **Unmarked, the politics of performance** (London and New York: Routledge, 1993): 146.

39. PHELAN: 148-149.

40. NEIDICH, "Neuropower."

heterogeneous sampling machine. As such, the summated condition of an unstable fluid social mind, the resultant of the combined dispositions of its individual members, is the true site of action of the virtuoso performance, which is now about the stabilization of anarchic dispositions in moments of synchronous appreciation. This, for Neidich, is the true condition of intensive culture that now acts to synchronize thought and consciousness. It is only in the last century with the emergence of intensive culture, computer and Internet technology, social networks and social orders, and the production of the multitude that new forms of biopower and administrative techniques have emerged.

7. Conclusion, Redistribution of the Sensible

If the now is about becoming, then the artist's task is "...concerned with aesthetic acts as configurations of experience that create new modes of sense perception and induce novel forms of political subjectivity."[41] Neidich's work, perhaps, reinforces the fact that artists have always created their own distributions of the sensible. Taking this as its curatorial subject, Neidich's recent exhibition project, The Re-distribution of the Sensible (Gallery Magnus Muller, Berlin, 2007), reminiscent of Michael Hardt and Tony Negri's 'society of control,' deals with the issue of sovereignty: "Sovereignty, utilizing the methods of the global marketplace with the help of scientific research on perception and cognition, has conspired in creating complex networks of attention, which allow for the manufacture of explicit 'connectedness' that today defines the distribution of the sensible. [...] These networks form a hegemonic cultural syntax, which is inscribed on society as a whole, producing new forms of subjectivity and, in the case of a world tuned into global media, a bounded multitude."[42] Artists, as well, utilizing their own historical referents, materials, processes, and performances, create "complex assemblages that together compete with institutional arrangements for the attention of the mind."[43] Again, this work is optimistic, concerned with an imagined future, not destined to be a repetition of the past.

"[T]he essence of politics consists in interrupting the distribution of the sensible by supplementing it with those who have no part in the perceptual coordinates of the community, thereby modifying the very aesthetic-political field of possibility.

[...] Those who have no name, who remain invisible and inaudible, can only penetrate the police order via a mode of subjectivization that transforms the aesthetic coordinates of the community by implementing the universal presupposition of politics: we are all equal. Democracy itself is defined by these intermittent acts of political subjectivization that reconfigure the communal distribution of the sensible."[44]

This is central to the argument of Neidich's Neuropower. In the end, the brain and its collaborator, the mind, are the products of a multiplicity of culturally formed congruencies to which they are coupled. On one extreme is the institutional understanding that produces 'people' as a homogenous entity, easily controlled and manipulated within the confines of the historic nation state. On the other extreme are the conditions of aesthetic production itself, which produces another distribution according to its own rules, manufactured by alternative methods. Both extremes and all that falls in between function to form the conditions of the brain/mind interface. The power of art operates through this redistribution of the sensible, in spite of the institutional tendency to co-opt. Redistributed sensibilities, produced by aesthetically driven systems, sculpt new forms of neural networks, attempting to make sense of a newly configured distribution. Potentials locked in older configurations are released. This newly organized neural substrate, as it is modeled upon the new conditions of culture itself, creates new possibilities for creativity and imagination, elaborating new forms of the image of thought.

41.   JACQUES RANCIÈRE, "Foreword,"
      The Politics of Aesthetics: 9.

42.   The Re-distribution of the Sensible,
      press release, Gallery Magus
      Muller, Berlin, 2007.

43.   The Re-distribution of the Sensible

44.   ROCKHILL, "Translator's
      Introduction: Jacques Rancière's
      Politics of Perception,": 3.

NEUROPOWER UP
Lia Gangitano

Highlights & Notes

2005 - 2009

dimension was also a response to this distribution. The reproduction of optical depth was linked to the privilege accorded to the *story*. In the Renaissance, the reproduction of three-dimensional space was involved in the valorization of painting and the assertion of its ability to capture an act of living speech, the decisive moment of action and meaning. In opposition to the Platonic degradation of *mimēsis*, the classical poetics of representation wanted to endow the 'flat surface' with speech or with a 'scene' of life, with a specific depth such as the manifestation of an action, the expression of an interiority, or the transmission of meaning. Classical poetics established [20] a relationship of correspondence at a distance between speech and painting, between the sayable and the visible, which gave 'imitation' its own specific space.

It is this relationship that is at stake in the supposed distinction between two-dimensional and three-dimensional space as 'specific' to a particular form of art. To a large extent, the ground was laid for painting's 'anti-representative revolution' by the flat surface of the page, in the change in how literature's 'images' function or the change in the discourse on painting, but also in the ways in which typography, posters, and the decorative arts became interlaced. The type of painting that is poorly named abstract, and which is supposedly brought back to its own proper medium, is implicated in an overall vision of a new human being lodged in new structures, surrounded by different objects. Its flatness is linked to the flatness of pages, posters, and tapestries. It is the flatness of an interface. Moreover, its anti-representative 'purity' is inscribed in a context where pure art and decorative art are intertwined, a context that straight away gives it a political signification. This context is not the surrounding revolutionary fever that made Malevich at once the artist who painted *Black Square* and the revolutionary eulogist of [21] 'new forms of life'. Furthermore, this is not some theatrical ideal of the new human being that seals the momentary alliance between revolutionary artists and politics. It is initially in the interface created between different 'mediums' – in the connections forged between poems and their typography or their illustrations, between the theatre and its set designers or poster designers, between decorative objects and poems – that this 'newness' is formed that links the artist who abolishes figurative representation to the revolutionary who invents a new form of life. This interface is

political in that it revokes the twofold politics inherent in the logic of representation. On the one hand, this logic separated the world of artistic imitations from the world of vital concerns and politico-social grandeur. On the other hand, its hierarchical organization – in particular the primacy of living speech/action over depicted images – formed an analogy with the socio-political order. With the triumph of the novel's page over the theatrical stage, the egalitarian intertwining of images and signs on pictorial or typographic surfaces, the elevation of artisans' art to the status of great art, and the new claim to bring art into the décor of each and every life, an entire well-ordered distribution of sensory experience was overturned.

[22] This is how the 'planarity' of the surface of depicted signs, the form of egalitarian distribution of the sensible stigmatized by Plato, intervened as the principle behind an art's 'formal' revolution at the same time as the principle behind the political redistribution of shared experience. The other major forms, among which there are those of the chorus and the theatre that I mentioned earlier, could be considered in much the same way. A history of aesthetic politics, understood in this sense, has to take into account the way in which these major forms stand in opposition to one another or intermingle. I am thinking, for example, of the way in which this paradigm of the surface of signs/forms entered into conflict or joined forces with the theatrical paradigm of presence, and with the diverse forms that this paradigm itself has taken on, from the Symbolist figuration of a collective legend to the actualized chorus of a new humanity. Politics plays itself out in the theatrical paradigm as the relationship between the stage and the audience, as meaning produced by the actor's body, as games of proximity or distance. Mallarmé's critical prose writings stage, in an exemplary manner, the play of cross-references, oppositions or assimilations between these forms, from the intimate theatre of the page and calligraphic choreography to the new 'service' performed by concerts.

[23] In one respect, these forms therefore appear to bring forth, in very different contexts, figures of community equal to themselves. However, they are susceptible to being assigned to contradictory political paradigms. Let us take the example of the tragic stage. It simultaneously carries with it, according to Plato, the syndrome of democracy and the power of illusion. By isolating *mimēsis* in its own proper space

---

of war, terror, and catastrophes of all kinds, at a level of production with which the artist with his artisan skills cannot compete. And in the meantime, politics has also shifted to the domain of media-produced imagery. Nowadays, every major politician generates thousands of images through public appearances. Correspondingly, politicians are now also increasingly judged on the aesthetics of their performance. This situation is often lamented as an indication that "content" and "issues" have become masked by "media appearance." But this increasing aestheticization of politics offers us at the same time a chance to analyze and to criticize the political performance in artistic terms. That is, media-driven politics operates on the terrain of art. At first glance the diversity of the media images may appear to be immense, if not nearly immeasurable. If one adds images of politics and war to those of advertising, commercial cinema, and entertainment, it seems that the artist—the last craftsperson of present-day modernity—stands no chance of rivaling the supremacy of these image-generating machines. But in reality, the diversity of images circulating in the media is highly limited. Indeed, in order to be effectively propagated and exploited in the commercial mass media, images need to be easily recognizable for the broad target audience, rendering mass media nearly tautological. The variety of images circulating in the mass media is much more limited than the range of images preserved, for example, in museums or produced by contemporary art. That is why it is necessary to keep the museums and, in general, art institutions as places where the visual vocabulary of the contemporary mass media can be critically compared to the art heritage of the previous epochs and where we can rediscover artistic visions and projects pointing toward the introduction of aesthetic equality.

Museums are increasingly being viewed today with skepticism and mistrust by both art insiders and the general public. On all sides one repeatedly hears that the institutional boundaries of the museum ought to be transgressed, deconstructed, or simply removed to give contemporary art full freedom to assert itself in real life. Such appeals and demands have become quite commonplace, to the extent of now being regarded as a cardinal feature of contemporary art. These calls for the abolition of the museum appear to follow earlier avant-garde strategies and as a result are wholeheartedly embraced by the contemporary art community. But appearances are deceiving. The context, meaning, and function of these calls to abolish the museum system

have undergone a fundamental change since the days of the avant-garde, even if at first sight the diction of these calls seems so familiar. Prevailing tastes in the nineteenth and the first part of the twentieth centuries were defined and embodied by the museum. In these circumstances, any protest directed at the museum was simultaneously a protest against the prevailing norms of art-making—and by the same token also the basis from which new, groundbreaking art could evolve. But in our time the museum has indisputably been stripped of its normative role. The general public now draws its notion of art from advertising, MTV videos, video games, and Hollywood blockbusters. In the contemporary context of media-generated taste, the call to abandon and dismantle the museum as an institution has necessarily taken on an entirely different meaning than when it was voiced during the avant-garde era. When people today speak of "real life," what they usually mean is the global media market. And that means: The current protest against the museum is no longer part of a struggle being waged against normative taste in the name of aesthetic equality but is, inversely, aimed at stabilizing and entrenching currently prevailing tastes.

Art institutions, however, are still typically portrayed in the media as places of selection, where specialists, insiders, and the initiated few pass preliminary judgment on what is permitted to rate as art in general, and what in particular is "good" art. This selection process is assumed to be based on criteria that to a wider audience must seem unfathomable, incomprehensible and, in the final estimation, also irrelevant. Accordingly, one wonders why anyone at all is needed to decide what is art and what is not. Why can't we just choose for ourselves what we wish to acknowledge or appreciate as art without looking to an intermediary, without patronizing advice from curators and art critics? Why does art refuse to seek legitimacy on the open market just like any other product? From a mass media perspective, the traditional aspirations of the museum seem historically obsolete, out of touch, insincere, even somewhat bizarre. And contemporary art itself time and again displays an eagerness to follow the enticements of the mass media age, voluntarily abandoning the museum in the quest to be disseminated through media channels. Of course, the readiness on the part of many artists to become involved in the media, in broader public communication and politics—in other words to engage in "real life" beyond the boundaries of the museum—is quite understandable. This kind of opening allows the artists to

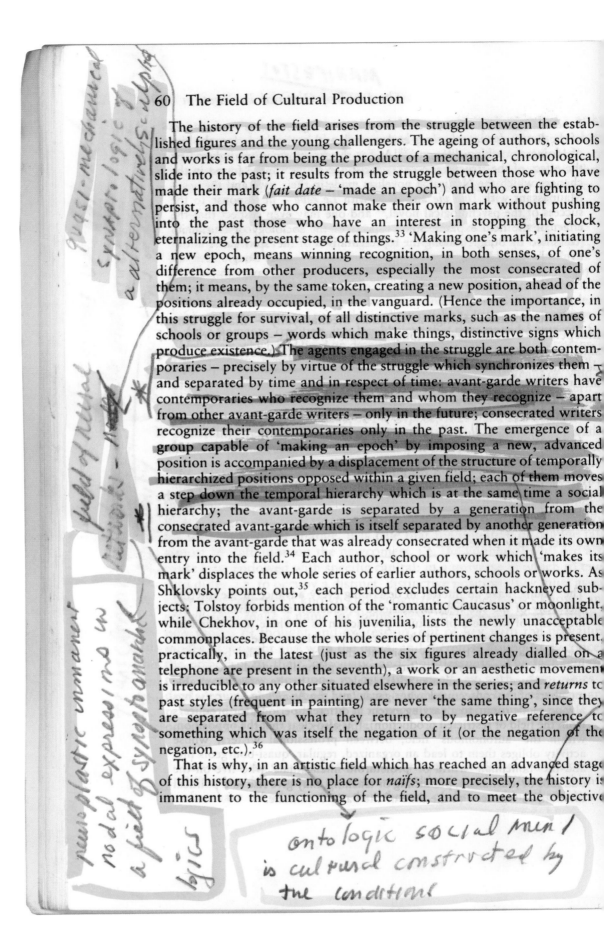

60 The Field of Cultural Production

The history of the field arises from the struggle between the established figures and the young challengers. The ageing of authors, schools and works is far from being the product of a mechanical, chronological, slide into the past; it results from the struggle between those who have made their mark (*fait date* – 'made an epoch') and who are fighting to persist, and those who cannot make their own mark without pushing into the past those who have an interest in stopping the clock, eternalizing the present stage of things.[33] 'Making one's mark', initiating a new epoch, means winning recognition, in both senses, of one's difference from other producers, especially the most consecrated of them; it means, by the same token, creating a new position, ahead of the positions already occupied, in the vanguard. (Hence the importance, in this struggle for survival, of all distinctive marks, such as the names of schools or groups – words which make things, distinctive signs which produce existence.) The agents engaged in the struggle are both contemporaries – precisely by virtue of the struggle which synchronizes them – and separated by time and in respect of time: avant-garde writers have contemporaries who recognize them and whom they recognize – apart from other avant-garde writers – only in the future; consecrated writers recognize their contemporaries only in the past. The emergence of a group capable of 'making an epoch' by imposing a new, advanced position is accompanied by a displacement of the structure of temporally hierarchized positions opposed within a given field; each of them moves a step down the temporal hierarchy which is at the same time a social hierarchy; the avant-garde is separated by a generation from the consecrated avant-garde which is itself separated by another generation from the avant-garde that was already consecrated when it made its own entry into the field.[34] Each author, school or work which 'makes its mark' displaces the whole series of earlier authors, schools or works. As Shklovsky points out,[35] each period excludes certain hackneyed subjects: Tolstoy forbids mention of the 'romantic Caucasus' or moonlight, while Chekhov, in one of his juvenilia, lists the newly unacceptable commonplaces. Because the whole series of pertinent changes is present, practically, in the latest (just as the six figures already dialled on a telephone are present in the seventh), a work or an aesthetic movement is irreducible to any other situated elsewhere in the series; and *returns* to past styles (frequent in painting) are never 'the same thing', since they are separated from what they return to by negative reference to something which was itself the negation of it (or the negation of the negation, etc.).[36]

That is why, in an artistic field which has reached an advanced stage of this history, there is no place for *naïfs*; more precisely, the history is immanent to the functioning of the field, and to meet the objective

< P. 25 / top
Highlights, Art Power, 2009,
highlighter and graphite,
22.8 x 29.5cm.

< P. 25 / bottom
Highlights, The Politics of Aesthetics,
2005, highlighter and blue ink,
19 x 26.7cm.

demands it implies, as a producer but also as a consumer, one has to possess the whole history of the field.[37]

Here it would be appropriate to point to the ideal-typical opposition between Rousseau and Duchamp. Rousseau, the painter as object, who does something other than what he thinks he is doing, does not know what he does, because he knows nothing of the field he stumbles into, of which he is the *plaything* (it is significant that his painter and poet 'friends' stage parodic consecration scenes for him); he is made by the field, a 'creator' who has to be 'created' as a legitimate producer, with the character of 'Douanier Rousseau', in order to legitimate his product.[38] By contrast, Duchamp, born into a family of painters, the younger brother of painters, has all the tricks of the artist's trade at his fingertips, i.e. an art of painting which (subsequently) implies not only the art of producing a work but the art of self-presentation; like the chess-player he is, he shows himself capable of thinking several moves ahead, producing art objects in which the production of the producer as artist is the precondition for the production of these objects as works of art; he admires Brisset as 'the Douanier Rousseau of philology' and invents the 'ready-made', a 'manu-factured object promoted to the dignity of an *objet d'art* by the symbolic authority of the artist' (quite unlike Rousseau, who makes 'assisted ready-mades' but shamefacedly conceals his sources, e.g. for *Le lion mangeant les explorateurs*); even when he uses mythical or sexual symbols, he refers to an esoteric, alchemical, mythological or psychoana-lytic culture; and he always situates himself at the second degree, even when he disabuses his exegetes of the sophisticated interpretations they have given of his works.

POSITIONS AND DISPOSITIONS

The Meeting of Two Histories

To understand the practices of writers and artists, and not least their products, entails understanding that they are the result of the meeting of two histories: the history of the positions they occupy and the history of their dispositions. Although position helps to shape dispositions, the latter, in so far as they are the product of independent conditions, have an existence and efficacy of their own and can help to shape positions. In no field is the confrontation between positions and dispositions more continuous or uncertain than in the literary and artistic field. Offering positions that are relatively uninstitutionalized, never legally guaran-teed, therefore open to symbolic challenge, and non-hereditary (al-though there are specific forms of transmission), it is the arena *par*

projection of these differences NOW INTERNALIZES

of the mutating conditions of the cultural discourse which produces new generational discourse fields as o (let us even say, the skeletal structure of it); they allow for the existence of every individual expression we use and they give structure to these expressions as well. Such "places" are *common* because no one can do without them (from the refined orator to the drunkard who mumbles words hard to understand, from the business person to the politician). Aristotle points out three of these "places": the connection between more and less, the opposition of opposites, and the category of reciprocity ("If I am her brother, she is my sister").

These categories, like every true skeletal structure, never appear as such. They are the woof of the "life of the mind," but they are an *inconspicuous* woof. What is it, then, that can actually be seen in the forms of our discourse? The "special places," as Aristotle calls them (*topoi idioi*). These are ways of saying something—metaphors, witticisms, allocutions, etc.—which are appropriate in one or another sphere of associative life. "Special places" are ways of saying/thinking something which end up being appropriate at a local political party headquarters, or in church, or in a university classroom, or among sports fans of a certain team. And so on. Whether it be the life of the city or its *ethos* (shared customs), these are articulated by means of "special places" which are different from one another and often incompatible. A certain expression might function in one situation and not in another; a certain type of argumentation might succeed in convincing one audience, but not another, etc.

The transformation with which we must come to terms can be summarized in this way: in today's world, the "special places" of discourse and of argumentation are perishing and dissolving, while immediate visibility is being gained by the "common places," or by generic logical-linguistic forms which establish the pattern for all forms of discourse. This means that in order to get a sense of orientation in the world and to protect ourselves from its dangers, we can not rely on those forms of thought, of reasoning, or of discourse which have their niche in one particular context or another. The clan of sports fans, the religious community, the branch of a political party, the workplace: all of these "places" obviously continue to exist, but none of them is sufficiently characterized or characterizing as to be able to offer us a wind rose, or a standard of orientation, a trustworthy compass, a unity of specific customs, of specific ways of saying/ thinking things. Everywhere, and in every situation, we speak/ think in the same way, on the basis of logical-linguistic constructs which are as fundamental as they are broadly general. An ethical-rhetorical topography is disappearing. The "common places" (these inadequate principles of the "life of the mind") are moving to the forefront: the connection between more and less,

36

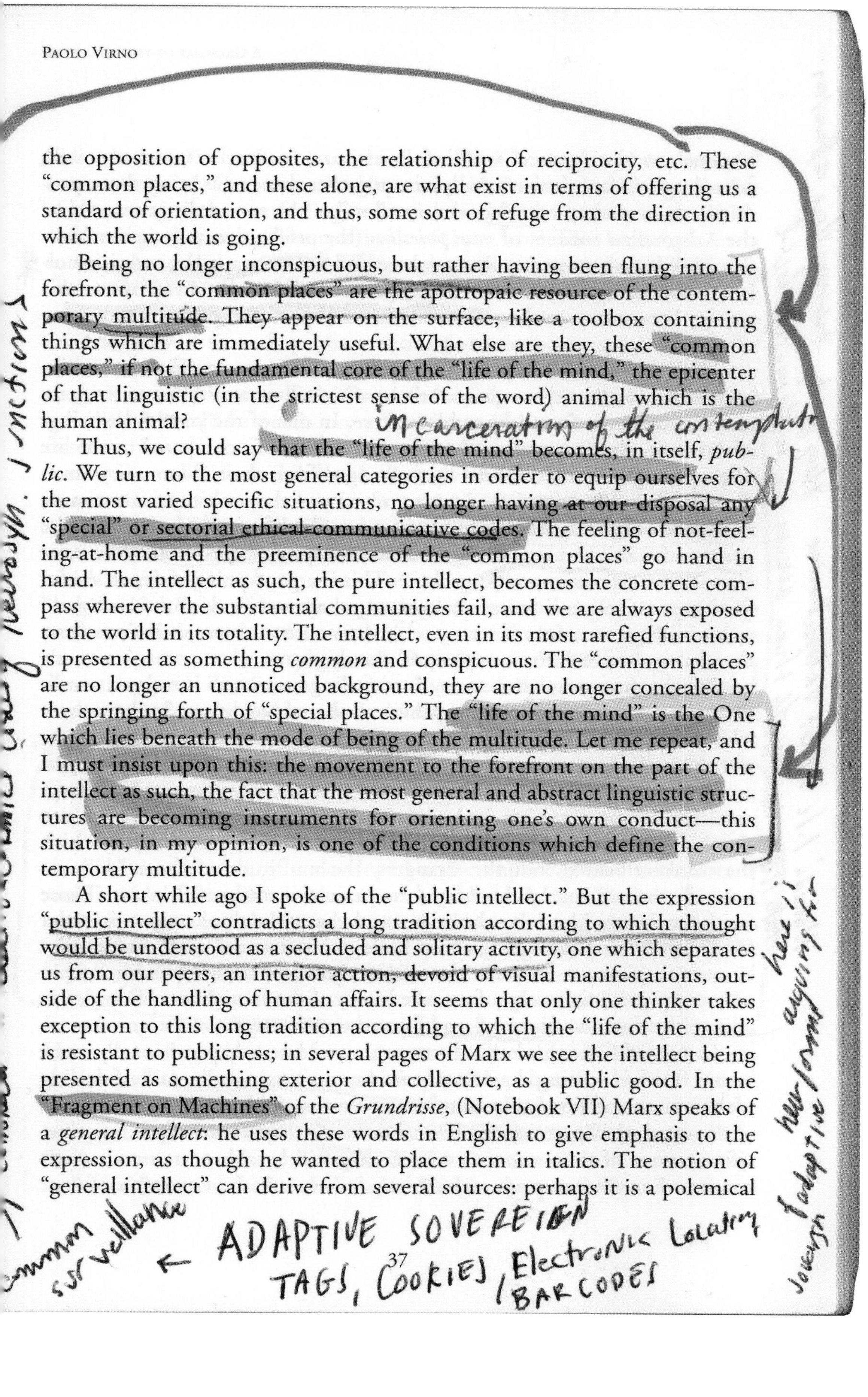

the opposition of opposites, the relationship of reciprocity, etc. These "common places," and these alone, are what exist in terms of offering us a standard of orientation, and thus, some sort of refuge from the direction in which the world is going.

Being no longer inconspicuous, but rather having been flung into the forefront, the "common places" are the apotropaic resource of the contemporary multitude. They appear on the surface, like a toolbox containing things which are immediately useful. What else are they, these "common places," if not the fundamental core of the "life of the mind," the epicenter of that linguistic (in the strictest sense of the word) animal which is the human animal?

Thus, we could say that the "life of the mind" becomes, in itself, *public*. We turn to the most general categories in order to equip ourselves for the most varied specific situations, no longer having at our disposal any "special" or sectorial ethical-communicative codes. The feeling of not-feeling-at-home and the preeminence of the "common places" go hand in hand. The intellect as such, the pure intellect, becomes the concrete compass wherever the substantial communities fail, and we are always exposed to the world in its totality. The intellect, even in its most rarefied functions, is presented as something *common* and conspicuous. The "common places" are no longer an unnoticed background, they are no longer concealed by the springing forth of "special places." The "life of the mind" is the One which lies beneath the mode of being of the multitude. Let me repeat, and I must insist upon this: the movement to the forefront on the part of the intellect as such, the fact that the most general and abstract linguistic structures are becoming instruments for orienting one's own conduct—this situation, in my opinion, is one of the conditions which define the contemporary multitude.

A short while ago I spoke of the "public intellect." But the expression "public intellect" contradicts a long tradition according to which thought would be understood as a secluded and solitary activity, one which separates us from our peers, an interior action, devoid of visual manifestations, outside of the handling of human affairs. It seems that only one thinker takes exception to this long tradition according to which the "life of the mind" is resistant to publicness; in several pages of Marx we see the intellect being presented as something exterior and collective, as a public good. In the "Fragment on Machines" of the *Grundrisse*, (Notebook VII) Marx speaks of a *general intellect*: he uses these words in English to give emphasis to the expression, as though he wanted to place them in italics. The notion of "general intellect" can derive from several sources: perhaps it is a polemical

37

incarceration of the contemplator
ADAPTIVE SOVEREIGN
TAGS, COOKIES, Electronic Locating, BAR CODES
common surveillance
here is arguing for new forms of adaptive sovereign

Highlights, A Grammar of the Multitude, 2007, highlighter and graphite, 22.7 x 29cm.

Modernity and Difference

A Conversation
between Stuart Hall
and Sarat Maharaj

Stuart Hall

As I think is true of all important terms in this kind of debate, it is best to deconstruct a term before you use it, or at least explain what you do not intend it to mean. There is one sense of the term 'translation' that I do not want to awaken, which is the notion that there is an original text and that all translations are then necessarily partial renderings of that original. They stand in relation to the original text as copies to origin. However, I'm really not interested in the notion of origin in that sense, because my position is that most original texts, when looked at closely, turn out to be translations themselves.

I regard translation as an unending process, a process without a beginning. Except in myth, there is no moment when cultures and identities emerge from nowhere, whole within themselves, perfectly self-sufficient, unrelated to anything outside of themselves and with boundaries which secure their space from outside intrusion. I do not think that either historically or conceptually we should think of cultures or identities or indeed texts in that way. Every text has a 'before-text', every identity has its pre-identities. I am not interested in the notion of translation in terms of rendering what has already been authentically and authoritatively fixed; what I want to do instead is to think of cultural practices as always involved in the process of translating.

Cultural processes do not have a pure beginning; they always begin with some irritant, some dirty or 'worldly' starting point, if I can call it that. When I say 'dirty', I mean that there is no pure moment of beginning; they are always already in flow and translation, therefore, is always from one idiom, language or ideolect into another. All languages have their own internal character, their own kind of ethos, their own space, and so it is therefore impossible to think of a perfect translation; no such thing exists. One has always to think of cultural production of any kind as a reworking, as inadequate to its foundations, as always lacking something. There is always something which is left out. There is always mistranslation because a translation can never be a perfect rendering from one space or one language to another. It is bound to be somewhat misunderstood, as we are all always misunderstood in every dialogue we undertake. There is no moment of dialogic relationship with an other which is perfectly understood by them in exactly the way intended by us, because translation is a mediation between two already constituting worlds. There is no perfect transparency.

So the notion of a perfect translation does not help us at all. What we usually think of as polarised between copying or mimicking on the one hand and the moment of pure creativity on the other are really two moments that are mutually constituting – they do not exist in a pure form. Pure creativity draws on something which is already there; it moves from one space to another and the creative act is that movement. It is not that I have thought of something or said something or produced something which has never been produced before – it is not the romantic notion of a pure start. Nor is it the notion of a pure finish, because every translation generates another. No-one reads a translation without thinking, 'I bet that's what the original really means. I bet I could express it better.'

One has to think of meaning as constituted by an infinite, incomplete series of translations. I think cultures are like that too, and so are identities. I think cultural production is like that and I am sure that texts are like that. In fact, the notion of 'cultural translation' is absolutely central to an understanding of this whole field. There are many people who have contributed to this particular notion of translation which I am trying to invoke, but I shall mention just three names as a way of orienting my argument: Walter Benjamin, Jacques Derrida and Mikhail Bakhtin.

Sarat Maharaj
Stuart has put the ideas across clearly with regard to cultural translation – I feel there is little more I could add, except simply to expand on what he has said and refer back to my essay on the untranslatable, since for me the search for translatability

37

Highlights, Modernity and Difference, 2006, highlighter and red ink, 22.6 x 32cm.

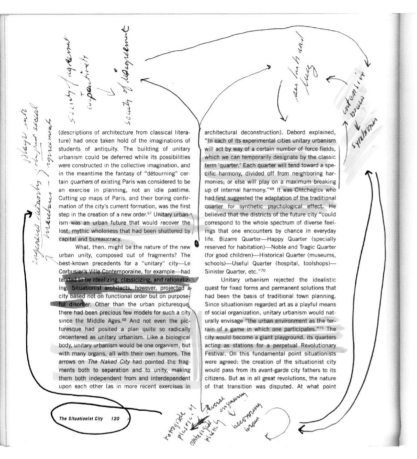

Highlights, The Situationist City,
2006, highlighter and ink,
23.3 x 41.6cm

Resistance is Futile / Resistance is Fertile

Kunsthaus Graz, Graz / Pro qm, Berlin, 2006

Resistance is Futile / Resistance
is Fertile, 2006, neon sculpture,
2 x 30', Kunsthaus Graz, Graz,
Austria.

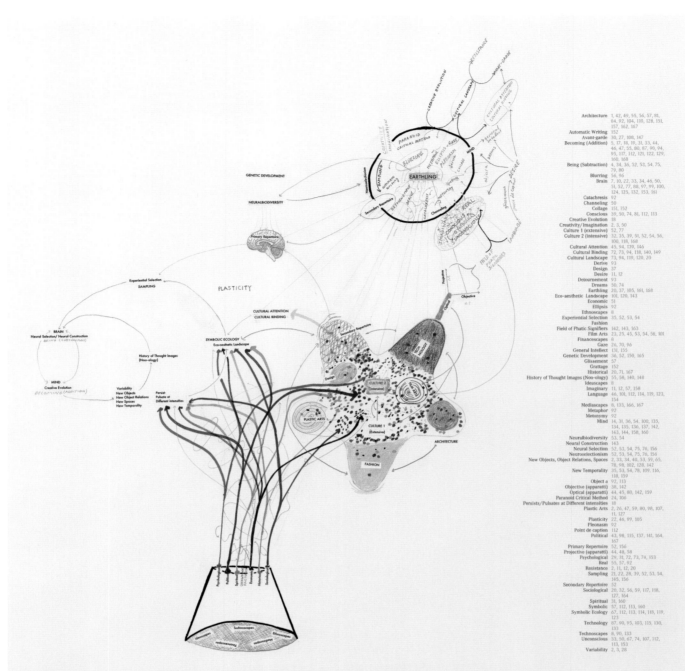

resistance is futile / resistance is fertile

1. Abbott, Edwin, Flatland, Princeton, 1991. 2. Adorno, Theodor W., Aesthetic Theory, trans. Robert Hullot-Kentor, Minneapolis, 1997. 3. Adorno, Theodor W., Minima Moralia: Reflections on a Damaged Life, London, 1991. 4. Adorno, Theodor W., The Culture Industry, London, 1991. 5. Agamben, Giorgio, The Open: Man and Animal, Stanford, 2004. 6. Agamben, Giorgio, Homo Sacer: Sovereign Power and Bare Life, Stanford, 1998. 7. Altman, John, Evolving Brains, New York, 1999. 8. Appadurai, Arjun, Modernity at Large: Cultural Dimensions of Globalization, Minneapolis, 2000. 9. Basar, Eral, Memory and Brain Dynamics: Oscillations Integrating Attention, Perception, Learning, and Memory, Boca Raton, 2004. 10. Bataille, Georges, Eroticism, Death and Sensuality, San Francisco, 1986. 11. Bataille, Georges, Visions of Excess, Selected Writings, trans. Allan Stoekl, Minneapolis, 1985. 12. Batchen, Geoffrey, Burning With Desire: The Conception of Photography, Cambridge, 1997. 13. Bateson, Gregory, Steps to an Ecology of Mind, Chicago, 1972. 14. Benjamin, Walter, Illuminations, London, 1999. 15. Benjamin, Walter, One Way Street, London, 1997. 16. Bergson, Henri, Matter and Memory, New York, 1988. 17. Bergson, Henri, Creative Evolution, New York, 1998. 18. Bergson, Henri, The Creative Mind: An Introduction to Metaphysics, New York, 2002. 19. Bhabha, Homi K., The Location of Culture, London, 1994. 20. Bizher, Stefan and Feverstein, Thomas, eds., Sample Minds: Materials on Sampling Culture, Cologne, 2005. 21. Boniface, Simon and Ziemann, Ulf, eds., Plasticity in the Human Nervous System: Investigations with Transcranial Magnetic Stimulator, New York, 2003. 22. Bordwell, David and Coward, Noel, Post-Theory: Reconstructing Film Studies, Madison, 1996. 23. Bosquet, Alain, Conversations with Salvador Dali, New York, 1969. 24. Braudy, Leo and Cohen, Marshall, Film Theory and Criticism, London, 1999. 25. Bryson, Norman, Vision and Painting: The Logic of the Gaze, New Haven, 1983. 26. Buchloh, Benjamin, H. D., Neo-Avantgarde and Culture Industry, Cambridge, 2006. 27. Bull, Michael and Back, Les, eds., The Auditory Culture Reader, New York, 2004. 28. Butler, David J., Adapting Minds, Evolutionary Psychology and the Persistent Quest, Cambridge, 2005. 29. Burger, Peter, Theory of the Avant-Garde, Minneapolis, 1984. 30. Caldwell, W. V., LSD Psychotherapy: An Exploration of Psychedelic and Psychedelic Therapy, New York, 1968. 31. Castells, Manuel, The Rise of the Network Society, Edinburgh, 1996. 32. Changeaux, Jean-Pierre and Chavaillon, Jean, eds., Origins of the Human Brain, Oxford, 1996. 33. Changeaux, Jean Pierre, Neuronal Man: The Biology of Mind, Princeton, 1985. 34. Changeaux, Jean Pierre, The Physiology of Truth: Neuroscience and Human Knowledge, London, 2004. 35. Churchland, Patricia, Neurophilosophy: Toward a Unified Science of the Mind-Brain, Cambridge, 1989. 36. Clarke, Arthur C., 2001: A Space Odyssey, London, 1997. 37. Clarke, Edwin and Jacyna, L.S., Nineteenth Century Origins of Neuroscientific Concepts, Berkeley, 1987. 38. Cleeremans, Axel, ed., The Unity of Consciousness: Binding, Integration and Dissociation, New York, 2003. 39. Cloke, Paul, and Johnston, Ron, eds., Spaces of Geographical Thought: Deconstructing Human Geography's Binaries, London, 2005. 40. Coles, Alex, The Optic of Walter Benjamin, Reading, 1999. 41. Colomina, Beatriz, Privacy and Publicity, Cambridge, 1996. 42. Connolly, William E., Neuropolitics: Thinking, Culture, Speed, Minneapolis, 2002. 43. Crary, Jonathan, Techniques of the Observer, Cambridge, 1990. 44. Crary, Jonathan, Suspensions of Perception: Attention, Spectacle, and Modern Culture, Cambridge, 1999. 45. Deacon, Terrence W., The Symbolic Species: The Co-evolution of Language and the Brain, New York, 1997. 46. De Bolla, Peter, The Education of the Eye: Painting, Landscape, and Architecture in Eighteenth Century Britain, Stanford, 2003. 47. Debord, Guy, Society of the Spectacle, Detroit, 1983. 48. Decourt, Jean-Gilles & Rahm, Philippe, Physiological Architecture, Basel, 2002. 49. Dehaene, Stanislas, ed., The Cognitive Neuroscience of Consciousness, London, 2001. 50. De Landa, Manuel, A Thousand Years of Nonlinear History, New York, 1997. 51. De Landa, Manuel, Intensive Science and Virtual Philosophy, London, 2002. 52. Deleuze, Gilles, Cinema 1, The Movement Image, Minneapolis, 1993. 53. Deleuze, Gilles, Cinema 2, The Time Image, Minneapolis, 1993. 54. Deleuze, Gilles, Difference and Repetition, Presses Universitaires de France, 1968. 55. Deleuze, Gilles, The Fold: Leibniz and the Baroque, Minneapolis, 1993. 56. Deleuze, Gilles, What is Philosophy?, London, 1994. 57. Deleuze, Gilles and Guattari, Felix, A Thousand Plateaus, Minneapolis, 1987. 58. Deleuze, Gilles and Guattari, Felix, What is Philosophy?, London, 1994. 59. Didi-Huberman, Georges, Invention of Hysteria: Charcot and the Photographic Iconography of the Salpetriere, London, 2003. 60. Dupouy, Emmanuel, Language, Brain, and Cognitive Development, Cambridge, 2001. 61. Edelman, Gerald, Neural Darwinism, New York, 1987. 62. Edelman, Gerald, Remembered Present, New York, 1994. 63. Edelman, Gerald M. and Tononi, Giulio, A Universe of Consciousness: How Matter Becomes Imagination, New York, 2000. 64. Eisenman, Peter, Barefoot on White-Hot Walls, ed. Peter Noever, Ostfildern, 2005. 65. Eisenman, Peter, Blurred Zones, Investigation of the Interstitial, New York, 2003. 66. Eisenman, Peter, Inside Out, Selected Writings 1963-1988, New Haven, 2004. 67. Flaxman, Gregory, ed., The Brain is the Screen: Deleuze and the Philosophy of Cinema. Minneapolis, 2000. 68. Follin, Frances, Embodied Visions: Bridget Riley, Op Art and the Sixties, New York, 2004. 69. Foster, Hal, ed., Vision and Visuality, New York, 1985. 70. Foucault, Michel, The Archaeology of Knowledge, London, 2005. 71. Freud, Sigmund, Totem and Taboo, London, 1950. 72. Freud, Sigmund, Civilization and its Discontents, trans. Joan Riviere, New York, 1994. 73. Freud, Sigmund, The Interpretation of Dreams, The Standard Edition, trans. James Strachey, New York, 1965. 74. Foster, Joachim M., Cortex and Mind: Unifying Cognition, New York, 2003. 76. Gazzaniga, Michael, The Cognitive Neurosciences, Cambridge, 1995. 77. Gideon, Sigfried, Space, Time and Architecture, Cambridge, 1967. 78. Goethe, Johann Wolfgang Von, Theory of Colours, Cambridge, 1970. 79. Gombrich, E.H., Art and Illusion, Princeton, 1961. 80. Graham, Dan, Two-Way Mirror Power: Selected Writings by Dan Graham on his Art, Cambridge, 1999. 81. Gregory, R.L., Eye and Brain: The Psychology of Seeing, London, 1966. 82. Grosz, Elizabeth, Space, Time, Perversion, London, 1995. 83. Grosz, Elizabeth, Architecture from the Outside, Cambridge, 2001. 84. Guattari, Felix, Chaosophy, New York, 1995. 85. Hammerstein, Peter, Genetic and Cultural Evolution of Cooperation, Cambridge, 2006. 120. Levy, Pierre, and Bononno, Robert, Becoming Virtual: Reality in the Digital Age, New York, 1998. 121. Lewis-Williams, David, The Mind in the Cave, London, 2002. 122. Lieberman, Philip, Human Language and Our Reptilian Brain, Cambridge, 2000. 123. Llinas, Rodolfo R., I of the Vortex: From Neurons to Self, Cambridge, 2001. 124. Llinas, Rodolfo R. and Churchland, Patricia, The Mind-Brain Continuum, Sensory Processes, Cambridge, 1996. 125. Luhmann, Niklas, Art as a Social System, trans. Eva M. Knodt, Stanford, 2000. 127. Lynn, Greg, Animate Form, Princeton, 1999. 128. Lyotard, Jean-Francois, The Inhuman, Stanford, 1988. 129. Lyotard, Jean-Francois, The Postmodern Condition: A Report on Knowledge, Manchester, 2004. 130. Mackenzie, Adrian, Transductions: Bodies and Machines at Speed, London, 2002. 131. Marijuan, Pedro C. ed., Cajal and Consciousness: Scientific Approaches to Consciousness on the Centennial of Ramon y Cajal's Birth, New York, 2001. 132. Massumi, Brian, Parables for the Virtual: Movement, Affect, Sensation, Raleigh, 2002. 133. Maturana, Humberto R. and Varela, Francisco, The Tree of Knowledge: The Biological Roots of Human Understanding, London, 1987. 134. Maurleau-Ponty, Maurice, The Primacy of Perception, Chicago, 1964. 135. Maurleau-Ponty, Maurice, Phenomenology of Perception, London, 1962. 136. Mbembe, Achille, On the Postcolony, Berkeley, 2001. 137. Minsky, Marvin, Society of Mind, New York, 1988. 138. Mirzoeff, Nicholas, ed., The Visual Culture Reader, London, 1998. 139. Mitchell, W.J. T., What Do Pictures Mean?, Chicago, 2005. 140. Negri, Antonio and Hardt, Michael, Empire, Cambridge, 2000. 141. Neidich, Warren, Blow-up: Photography, Cinema and the Brain, New York, 2003. 142. Neidich, Warren, Earthling, New York, 2005. 143. Noe, Alva, ed., Is the World a Grand Illusion, London, 2002. 144. Nyman, Michael, Experimental Music: Cage and Beyond, Cambridge, 1981. 145. Pashler, Harold E., The Psychology of Attention, Cambridge, 1998. 146. Poggioli, Renato, The Theory of the Avant-Garde, Cambridge, 2003. 147. Rajchman, John, The Deleuze Connections, Cambridge, 2000. 148. Reyna, Stephen P., Connections: Brain, Mind, and Culture in Social Anthropology, London, 2002. 149. Richerson, Peter I. and Boyd, Robert, Not By Genes Alone, Chicago, 2005. 150. Rowe, Colin and Koetter, Fred, Collage City, Cambridge, 1984. 151. Rubin, William S., Dada, Surrealism and Their Heritage, The Museum of Modern Art, New York, 1968. 152. Solms, Mark and Turnbull, Oliver, The Brain and The Inner World: An Introduction to the Neuroscience of Subjective Experience, New York, 2002. 153. Saussure, Ferdinand, Course in General Linguistics, trans. Wade Baskin, New York, 1966. 154. Simondon, Gilbert, Du Mode d'existence des Objets Techniques, Paris, 1995. 155. Sporns, Olaf and Tononi Giulio, eds., Selectionism and the Brain, London, 1994. 156. Sprytwork, Lars, NOX: Machining Architecture, London, 2004. 157. Stafford, Barbara Maria, Visual Analogy: Consciousness as the Art of Connecting, Cambridge, 1999. 158. Stiegler, Bernard, Technics and Time 1: The Fault of Epimetheus, Stanford, 1998. 159. Varela, Francisco J., Thompson, Evan, and Rosch, Eleanor, The Embodied Mind, Cambridge, 1993. 160. Van Ooyen, Arjen, ed., Modeling Neural Development, Cambridge, 2003. 161. Vidler, Anthony, Warped Space: Art, Architecture, and Anxiety in Modern Culture, Cambridge, 2000. 162. Virilio, Paul, The Vision Machine, London, 1994. 163. Virno, Paolo, and Bertoletti, Isabella, The Grammar of the Multitude, New York, 2004. 164. Weber, Bruce B. and Depew, David J., eds., Evolution and Learning: The Baldwin Effect Reconsidered, Cambridge, 1990. 166. Zizek, Slavoj, Welcome to the Desert of the Real, London, 2002. 167. Zizek, Slavoj, Organs Without Bodies: On Deleuze and Consequences, London, 1994. 165. Williams, Raymond, Television, London, 1994.

WARREN NEIDICH AT PROQM OCTOBER 1 TILL NOVEMBER 5, 2006, THEMATISCHE BUCHHANDLUNG, ALTE SCHOENHAUSER STRASSE 48, D-10119 BERLIN, TEL. (030) 247 28520, FAX (030) 247 28521, MO.-FR. 12-20 UHR, SA. 12-18 UHR, INFO@PRO-QM.DE, WWW.PRO-QM.DE

Resistance is Futile / Resistance
is Fertile, 2006, poster, 60 x 85cm.

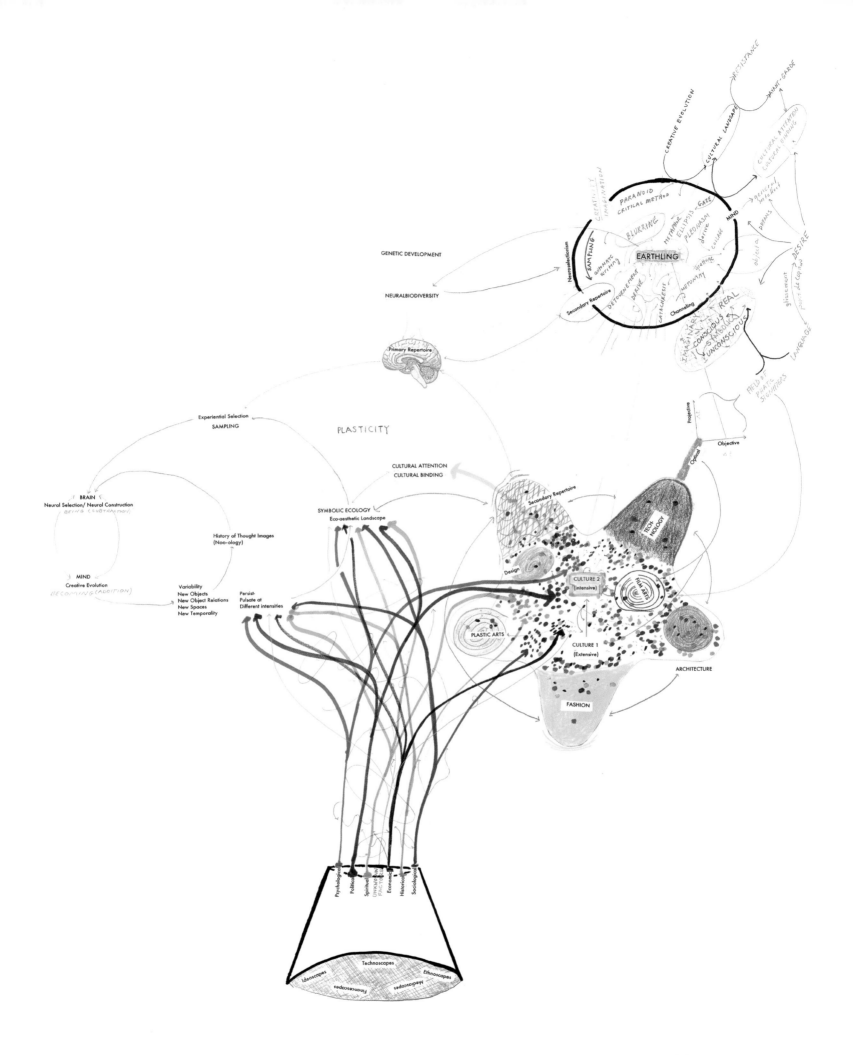

GENETIC DEVELOPMENT

NEURALBIODIVERSITY

EARTHLING

PLASTICITY

Experiential Selection
SAMPLING

CULTURAL ATTENTION
CULTURAL BINDING

BRAIN
Neural Selection/ Neural Construction
BEING (SUBTRACTION)

SYMBOLIC ECOLOGY
Eco-aesthetic Landscape

History of Thought Images
(Noo-ology)

MIND
Creative Evolution
BECOMING (ADDITION)

Variability
New Objects
New Object Relations
New Spaces
New Temporality

Persist-
Pulsate at
Different intensities

Secondary Repertoire

Primary Repertoire

TECH-
NOLOGY

Design

CULTURE 2
(intensive)

FILM
ARTS

PLASTIC ARTS

CULTURE 1
(Extensive)

ARCHITECTURE

FASHION

PARANOID
CRITICAL METHOD

BLURRING

Psychological
Political
Spiritual
UNKNOWN
FACTOR
Economic
Historical
Sociological

Ideoscapes
Technoscapes
Ethnoscapes
Financescapes
Mediascapes

> P. 38-40
Resistance is Futile / Resistance
is Fertile, 2006, poster, street
installation, Berlin.

Political Art of the Sixties was About Delineation, Political Art Today is About Differentiation

IASPIS, Stockholm, Sweden, 2008

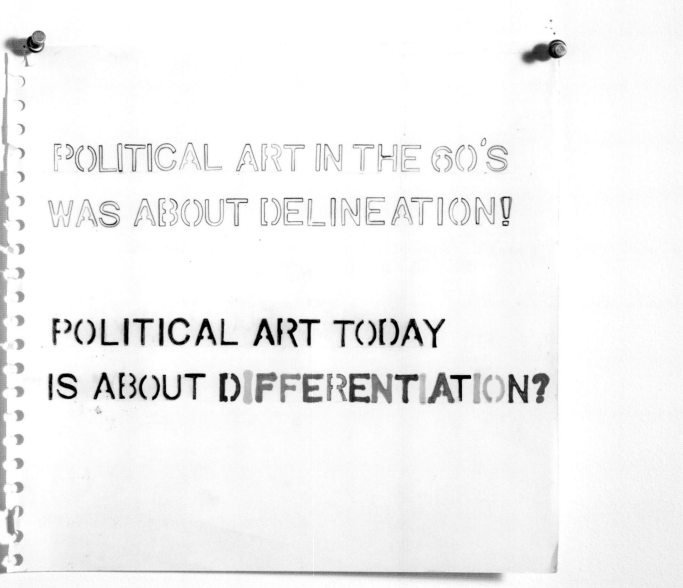

POLITICAL ART IN THE 60'S
WAS ABOUT DELINEATION!

POLITICAL ART TODAY
IS ABOUT DIFFERENTIATION?

Political Art in the 60's was about
Delineation, Political Art Today is
About Differentiation, 2008,
graphite and magic marker on paper,
28 x 27.9cm.

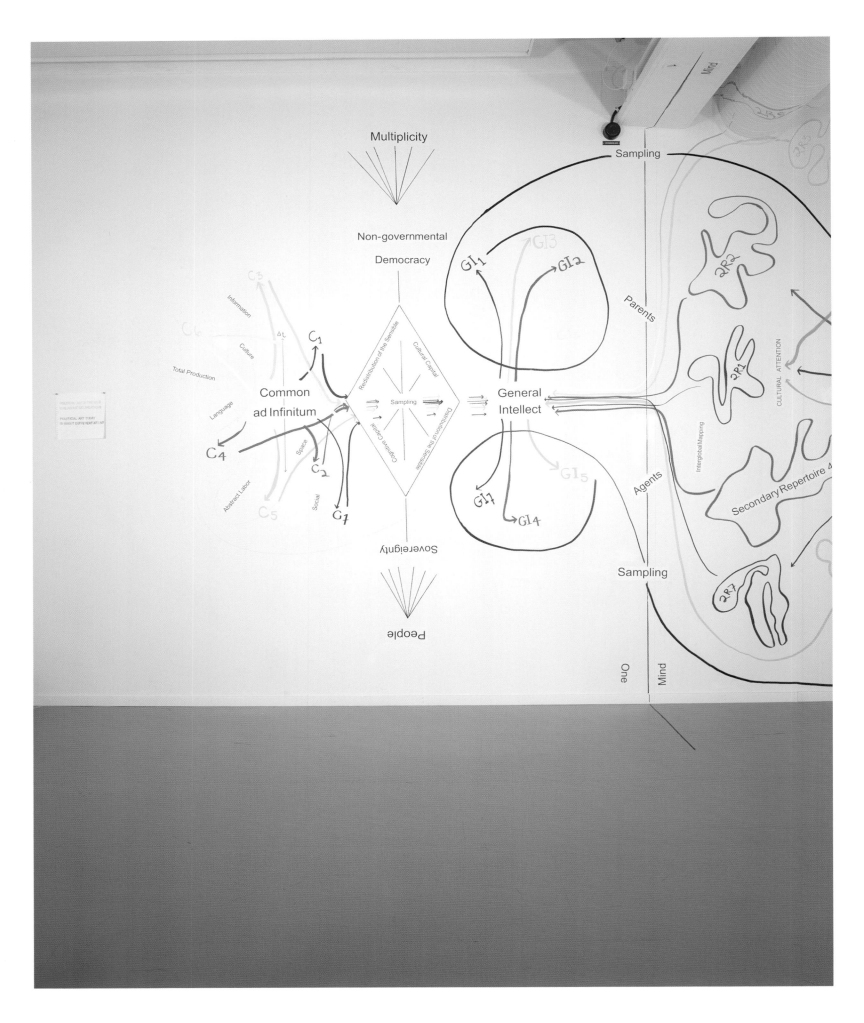

Political Art in the 60's was about Delineation, Political Art Today is About Differentiation, 2008, wall drawing with pen, ink, magic marker, paint markers, paper and tape, 10 x 3.5 m, composite view.

Mapping

Primary Repertoire

Brain Modifiability Ratio

Neurobiologic Common

Neurobiologic Diversity
History of Species

PLASTICITY

Secondary Repertoire

DÉTOURNE

IMAGINARY   REAL

CONSCIOUS
SYMBOLIC
UNCONSCIOUS

LANGUE

FIELD of
PHATIC
SIGNIFIERS

Projective

Objective

Secondary Repertoire

TECHNOLOGY

DESIGN

CULTURE 2
(intensive)

FILM

SYMBOLIC ECOLOGY

Eco-aesthetic Landscape

PLASTIC ARTS

CULTURE 1
(extensive)

ARCHITECTURE

FASHION

Psychology
Ethics

Ethnoscapes

Technoscapes

Ideoscapes

Financescapes

Mediascapes

IASPIS installation view

45

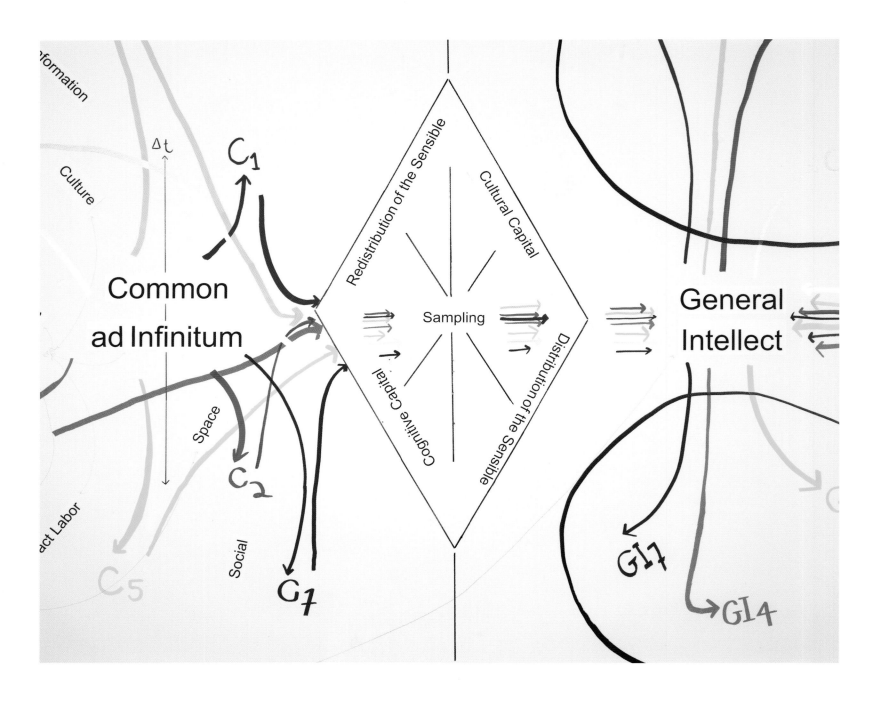

SYMBOLIC E

Eco-aesthetic L

COLOGY

ndscape

Neurobiologic Div

=

History of Spec

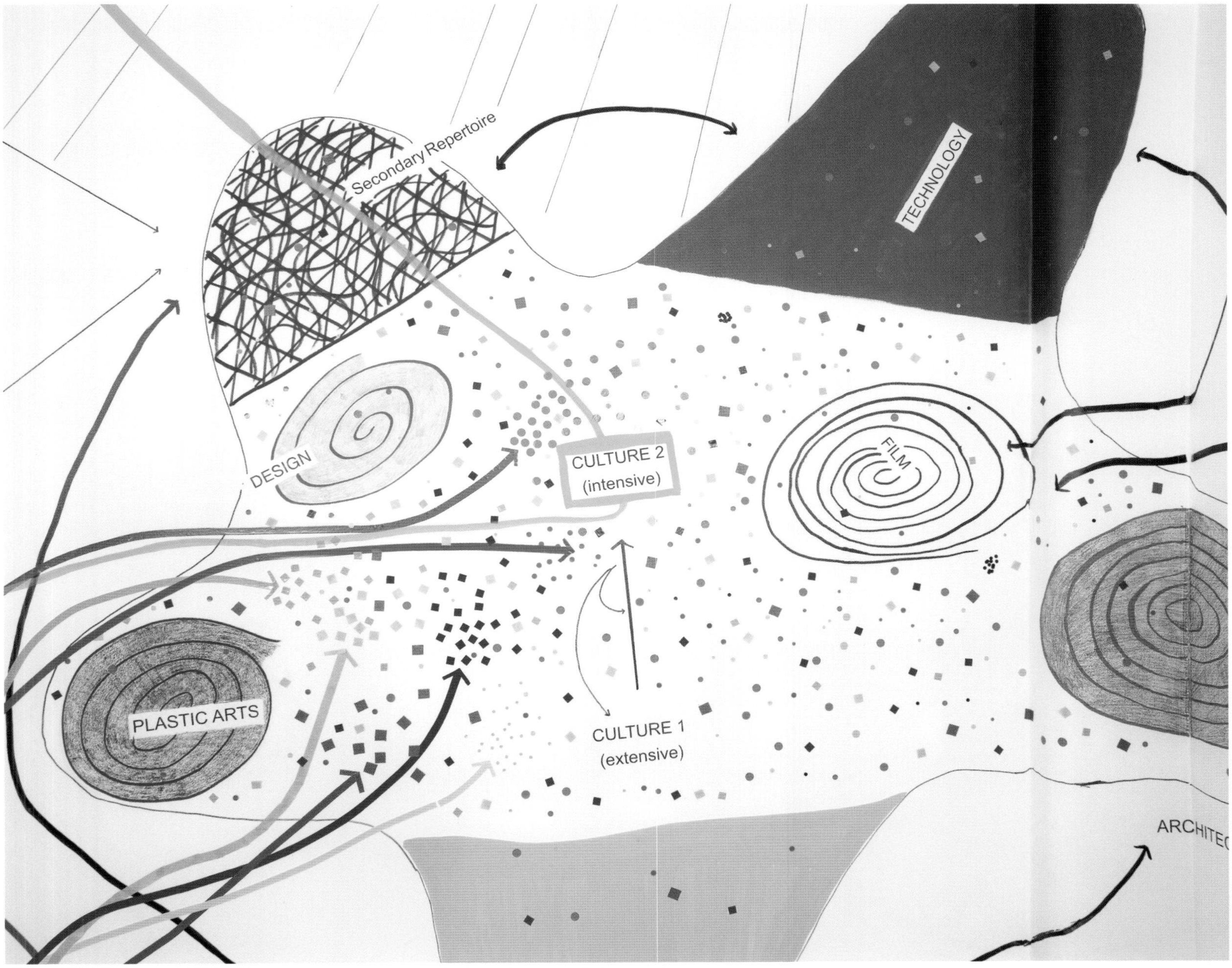

Secondary Repertoire
TECHNOLOGY
DESIGN
CULTURE 2
(intensive)
FILM
PLASTIC ARTS
CULTURE 1
(extensive)
ARCHITEC

Political Art in the 60's was about Delineation, Political Art Today is About Differentiation, 2008, (IASPIS), wall drawing with pen, ink, magic marker, paint markers, paper and tape, 10 x 3.5 m, detail.

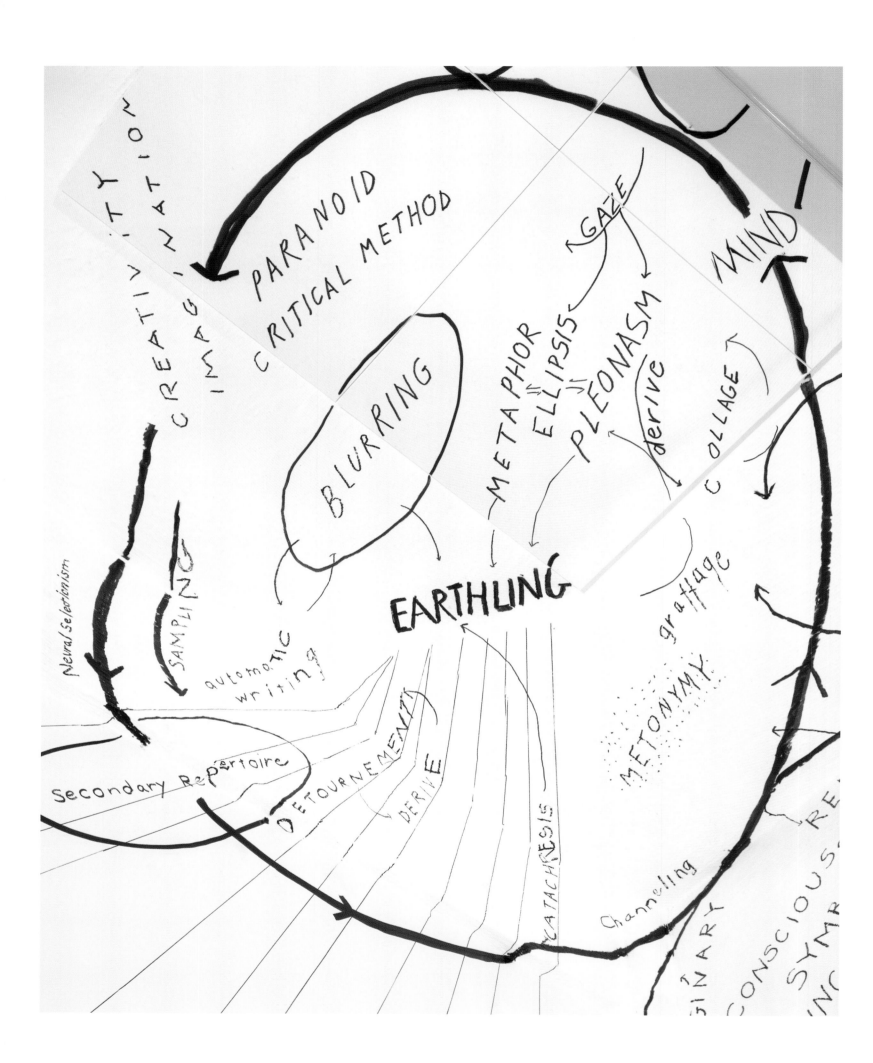

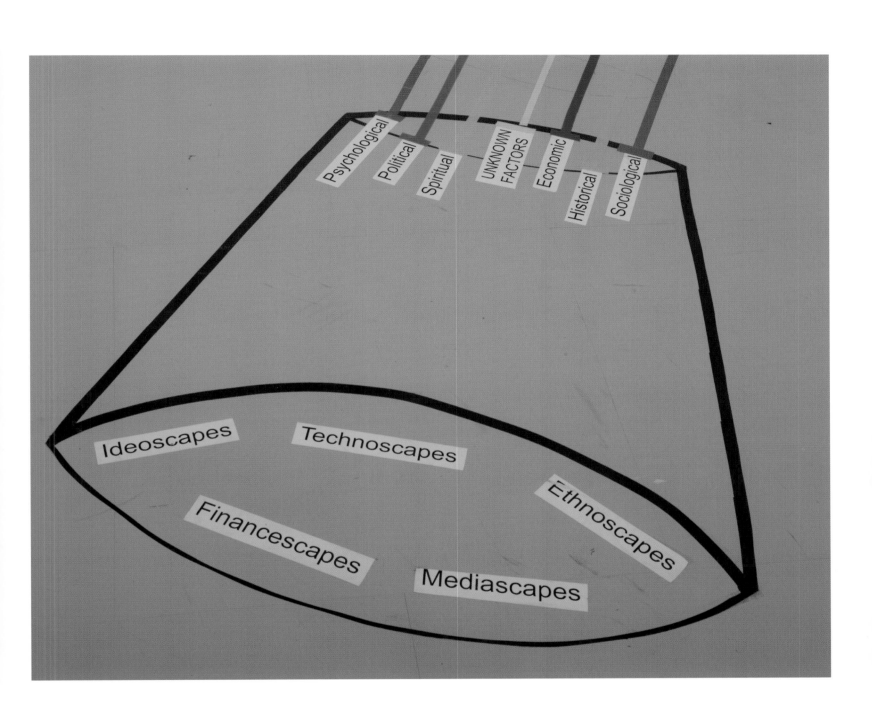

Psychological Political Spiritual UNKNOWN FACTORS Economic Historical Sociological

Ideoscapes Technoscapes Ethnoscapes Financescapes Mediascapes

Political Art in the 60's was about
Delineation, Political Art Today
is About Differentiation, 2008,
(IASPIS), wall drawing with pen,
ink, magic marker, paint markers,
paper and tape, 10 x 3.5 m, detail.

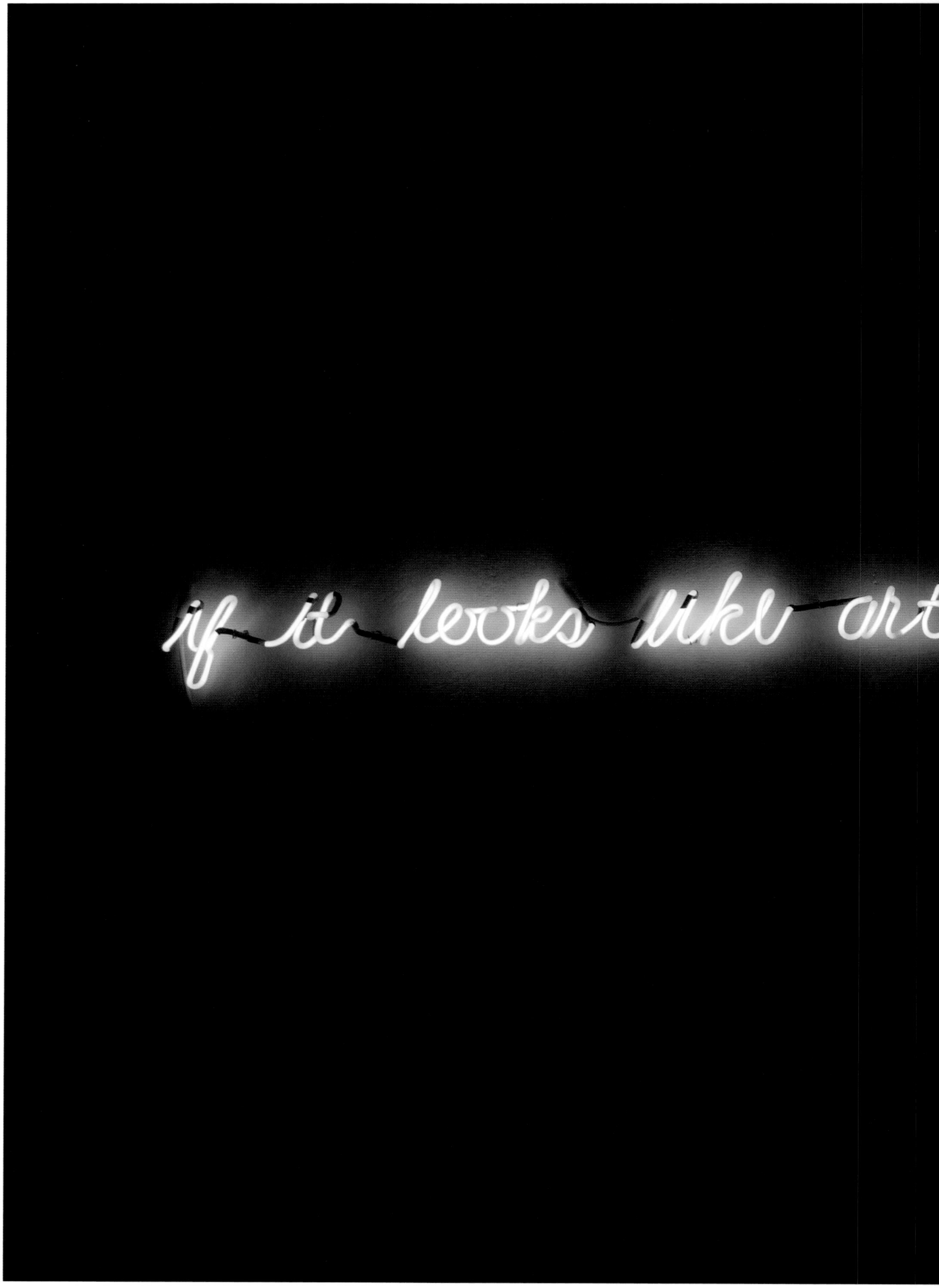
if it looks like art

If it looks like art it
probably isn't, 2008-9,
white neon, 2.5 x 0.15m.

Some Cursory Comments On the Nature of My Diagram- matic Drawings

IASPIS, Stockholm, Sweden, 2008

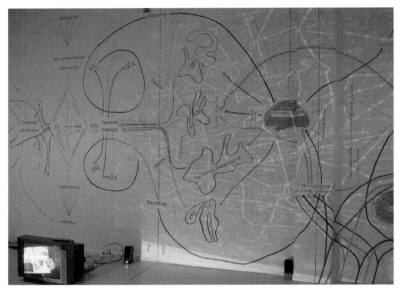

Some Cursory Comments on the Nature of My Wall Drawing, 2008, documentation of the performance and questions and answers afterwards, IASPIS, color video still.

Some Cursory Comments on the Nature
of My Wall Drawing, 2008,
performance documentation, IASPIS,
color video still.

Pointings

The diagram is indeed a chaos a catastrophe but it is also a germ of order or rhythm. It is a violent chaos in relation to the figurative givens, but it is a germ of rhythm in relation to the new order of the painting. As Bacon says, it "unlocks areas of sensation.

GILLES DELEUZE, Francis Bacon: The Logic of Sensation, 102.

The diagram or abstract machine is the map of relations between forces, a map of destiny, or intensity, which proceeds by primary non-localizable relation and at every moment passes through every point, or rather in every relation from one point to another.

GILLES DELEUZE, Foucault, 36.

Fig. 1

EARTHLING DRAWING:
TO READ IT IS TO PERFORM IT

I approach the Earthling Drawing that is tacked to my wall. It is at some distance now and what I see is a multicolored abstract drawing that covers the paper with lines, marks and points distributed unevenly. Several separate areas are demarcated like small continents. These parts, of which there are four, have developed over the past eight years. They have been drawn, overdrawn, redrawn extended and edited. They have existed on paper, as wall drawings and finally here as an immaterial projection work filling the void of the gallery. As such the drawing is an impermanent condition of a still evolving process! The first part is called the Cultured Brain Drawing and fills the space in the middle lower right hand section. It looks like an amoeba with pseudo pods. The second part is called the Global Generator. It is funnel shaped and situated at the bottom and sends out two outcroppings of colored tendrils that split according to very different logics one flowing into the Cultured Brain Drawing and the other into the third section which is called the Becoming Brain Drawing. That section, as we will see as this story unfolds, delineates the ways by which information culture as an epigenetic force produces changes in the way the brain and mind are configured. The Earthling Drawing is found in the upper right hand corner. Along with the General Intelligence Drawing at the far left it delineates how immaterial labor and Neoliberal global capitalism have produced new distributed networked dispositfs to administrate the subject at the conscious and unconscious level.

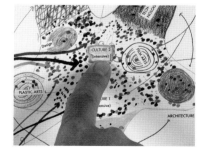

Fig. 2

As I continue my approach I realize that there are words that adorn it's arabesque forms. I first point and then deliver my finger quite randomly to a location towards the center left center. (I might add that this idea of pointing was woven into an intricate methodology called Detournement by the Situationists which produced new mappings of the city of Paris and at the same time conjured up the conditions, first described by the great Russian Psychologist Lev Vygotsky,

through which parents acting as agents help produce the conditions of attention in the child during his or her socialization process.) This initial touch begins a drifting process in which my finger-tip acting as a compass navigates a route or root to other locations and places as a tracing. My finger alights first in the Cultured Brain Drawing on Culture 1 (Extensive Culture). It then moves up along a tracing connecting it to Culture 2 (Intensive Culture). The arrow is bidirectional and connotes that each is symbiotic and contained in the other as nested symbolic gestures.

Fig. 3

Intensive Culture is the product of an ontologic process that emanates from Culture 1 (Extensive Culture) and is defined by multiplicitous, non-linear, rhizomatic processes, immaterial labor as a virtuoso performance and the conditions of the social brain. It has supplanted its predecessor Culture 1 (Extensive,Culture) defined here as a set of conditions which has been formed according to a different set of coordinates and logics. This is not to say that it has displaced it completely. In fact the two are simultaneously operational in this global social economy. Extensive logics as they concern, for instance, architecture are based on a homogenized geographical spread like that found in Courbusier's identical units of habitation and the grid city model of New York. Extensive labor is the model of the 19th century production of real objects tethered to the actions of the physical body working along an assembly line. It is driven on one hand by Karl Marx's idea of commodity and on the other by the rational bureaucracy of Max Weber. Intensive culture on the other hand is the culture of the network. Extensive culture is driven by the production of exact objects and is a culture of equivalence. Intensive culture on the other hand is one characterized by inequivalence and difference. Intensive things are one-offs and singular. Whereas extensive cultures produce the commodity as a form of equivalence, intensive culture is described best by the idea of the brand. Each brand is different from every other brand and the brand does not produce commodities but gives them value and enriches them through a vast array of connected externalities. In fact, the unseen and secret relations that each brand connotes, the complicated and intense backstage conditions of the information society are now subject themselves to quantification and analysis in the overall strategy of the administration of attention. The Ad Man or the Org man is as interested in the unseen affects of a marketing cam-

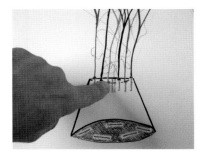

Fig. 4

paign, those that the ad was not initially supposed to interest, as they are on the targeted audience. Each is situated in a diffuse milieu of the Cultured Brain Drawing signified by random colored dots made with the end of a blunt magic markers, which are diffusely distributed throughout.

Closer inspection unveils a series of flowing multicolored lines swooping in from the bottom left where after entering the inside of the cultured brain section of the drawing they seem to fragment. By a reverse tracing the finger follows the multiple multi colored curved lines back down towards an upside down cone shaped funnel situated below. The cone is divided into two parts. The top is the generative source of the colored lines and upon close inspection one notices that they are labeled according to the social, political, historical, economic and psychological relations that they designate. Each, in-itself, is in a state of constant flux and becoming caused, on the one hand, by the incessant shifting of internal differences which form its structure constituted by, for instance, the logic of the symbolic conditions that give it meaning and on the other by the effect of the other proximate relations upon it. Moving the eye along each sinewy strand, in fact the eye has learned to follow the finger, one begins to notice lightly traced eddies and whirlpools that represent feedback and feedforward circuits that link all the relations together and which, through a series of tight junctions, open conduits which allow for the exchange of internalized elements. Information as it diffuses from one relation to the other, like that from the social to the political field, to refer to the notion first elaborated by Pierre Bourdieu, produce emergent differences that need to be adjusted to. Forming the substructure

of the funnel are a series of labels like Ethnocape and Mediascape that refer to the mutating conditions of intensive culture in the global setting adopted from the work of Arjun Appadurai, <u>Modernity at Large: Cultural Dimensions of Globalization</u>. They form the foundation of the cultural shifts from Culture 1 to Culture 2.

I resume my drift and now move my finger again upward and rejoin the The Cultured Brain Drawing. My finger tip like a vagabond circulates throughout the terrain of the inside finding shelter under its nested regularities labeled plastic arts, architecture, technology and the film arts. Each is a specific register of the history of its own development in the context of a milieu of changing contingencies. Each attempts, as best it can, using its own histories, performances, apparatti, techniques and materials to produce its own form of image. (For the sake of simplicity I am restricting myself here to Visual Culture.) This image, by which I mean a kind of composite of all images registered at a specific moment in time that together act to define an epoch, operates in the present and past tense simultaneously. It represents a series of decisions made by the ancestors of that culture which is reflected in the history of all its past images as each travels along its own journey of time. How much the design of jewelry and religious artifacts used in burial rights has changed since the time of the Cro Magna. In the present moment each is the consummated activity of all the immaterial relations that it embodies and which reflect back upon itself to be cognated by the subject as observer who, upon witnessing these differences in that ontology, understands these changes inherent in himself or herself. But as an assemblage of constitutive elements in the much larger apparatus of visual culture these separate forms together constitute non-linear, emerging forms that are together more then the sum of their parts. It is from these conditions, as they move away from equilibrium, that new forms emerge that begin to define an age. Thus who would have ever imagined that Surrealism would emerge from the Bowels of Impressionism and that the new Figuration of, say, John Currin or Elizabeth Peyton, would have developed in a culture obsessed with conceptualism and abstraction? And today, that the mutating social, political, historical, economic and psychological conditions of, for instance, Post-Fordist Labor in the Age of the Multitude and the Empire constitute the conditions of a new landscape of art works, built spaces, buildings and films that respond to these mutating condi-

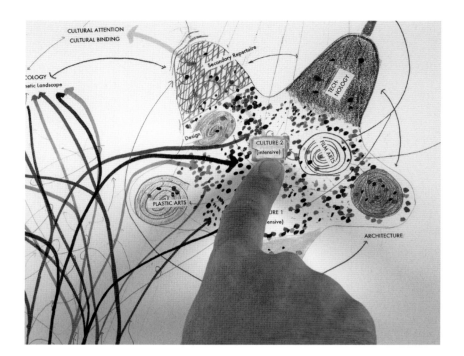

Fig. 5

tions, producing the works of Thomas Demand, Liam Gillick or Carey Young.

My finger, like a mouse on a computer screen, engages the drawing again now in a random walk through this information map and alights, after it moves through a portal, into an area called the Secondary Repertoire. The Secondary Repertoire is a condition of the nervous system which results from its reaction with the environment of which culture plays an ever more important role. As a result of the genetic contribution of your mother and father, which includes the genetic history of the species and the events of intrauterine development, the brain at birth is constituted by an array of neural elements that are ready to operate in the environment that the baby might find itself. In the human child at birth this nervous system is in a very open and immature state. He or she is born with a number of simple a priori wired reflexes like the sucking reflex which allow it to interact with its mother. I might say, however, that judged against other species this a priori brain is very underdeveloped compared to say a baby horse that at birth can already walk. However this is also a Becoming Brain, one that has a potential to be modified. According to Neuroscientists like Gerald Edelman, the brain is also made up of a large population of variable nervous elements some of which can become selected by the conditions of the world that it finds itself in. The process of, for instance, Neural Selectionism combined with the brains inherent potential for change, called Neural Plasticity, allows for a sculpting of the brain. Each culture provides a metaphor for that sculpting whether it be the Figurations of Rodin, the Scatter Art of Barry Le Vay or the cacophonous meanderings of Jason Rhodes

that call out to the brain in different ways intensifying different networks and currents. D.O. Hebb's famous adage of "Neurons that fire together Wire together" in this context becomes 'Network conditions in the Real-Imaginary-Virtual Interface sculpt Network Conditions in the Brain'. These new forms of interconnection reflect the cultural conditions and their immaterial relations which we already saw produced. These assemblages of Neural Networks as they are produced by the mutating conditions of culture create new potentials for thought and the imagination. In fact each culture adds to what Deleuze called Noo-ology, the history of the Thought Image, through its inflection in the intergenerational conditions of the selected brain and the psychological and philosophical thoughts that consequently emerge.

As we have mentioned already, Culture 2 directly contacts the Secondary Repertoire through a portal cut in the flesh of the diffuse milieu of Cultured Brain Drawings Microscopy. It is connected to the Primary Repertoire from which it emerges. The pluripotential Primary Repertoire, is the brain at birth or shortly before. It is the end point of Developmental Selection, which we mentioned above, and produces the variable population of neurons that Culture 2 can now act upon. It is a node that indirectly connects the other parts of the drawing; to its upper right the Earthling Drawing and to the left the Becoming Brain. The Earthling Drawing delineates the conditions of the unconscious and the pre-individual where the new logics of global Capitalism, according to Antonio Negri and Maritzio Lazzarato, are now focused. In the transformation of Labor to its current

Post-Fordist condition Noo-politics, the ensemble of techniques of control exercised on the brain and aimed at memory and attention, is the order of the day. Through the Distribution of Sensible, the <u>Partage du Sensible as Ranciere</u> has defined it, Soveriengty creates a series of laws and dispositions that establishes the modes of perception. The set of perceptual horizons, a system of self-evident facts of perception that delineates what can be heard, said, made and done. Those distributions are very different in an Intensive Culture then in an Extensive Cuture. The order and sequencing of those stimuli especially as they are generated in built space have implications for the history of the thought image and the becoming brain. In the present Intensive Global Culture the expanded role of capital in the generation of the general intellect consortiums of media giants, cognitive neuroscientific research assemblages, the military, advertising firms and polling interests consciously or unconsciously have littered Cultural Visual/Haptic Landscape with very sensational stimuli. We must see architecture and built space in an expanded way, not simply related to the paved streets and building facades that made up the Extensive City but, in the context of fields of immaterial gestures that form the new horizons of space and time. Paul Virilio has labeled these processed and engineered stimuli 'Phatic Stimuli' to draw attention to the conditions of Emphasis and Empathy, which are produced to call out to the brain and mind of the multitude. In extensive culture these stimuli were representational and manifested themselves in the here and now and specify specific commodities. Intensive culture is characterized by the brand. Brands are not actual they are virtual, not material but immaterial, not visible but invisible, and as such they actualize commodities bringing forth their full potential. In the intensive environment of self-reflexive global culture, one in which like this mental map featured here, in which one thing flows into the other, the possibility for feed-forward and feed-back looping becomes preeminent. Branded images are part of branded environments made up of series of branded networks. In intensive culture the mechanisms of the formation of these networks takes on center stage. These now Machinic Assemblages, as refered to by Gilles Deleuze, or as I refer to them Networks of Phaticity, are very powerful producers and modifiers of attention. In fact, according to this argument, their affect on attention is reflected back into the brain as they affect what memories are stored. (Although unconscious memories are also indirectly produced through, as we mentioned before, networks of externalities.) Phatic Stimuli, as they circulate in the real abstract conditions of billions of T.V. and computer desk top terminals, form intensive networks of phaticity and a simulated ecology of meaning becomes possible. This intensive environment is now what calls out to the brain and preferentially selects neurons and neural nets according to its logic. It is these networks that form the new architectures of today and which are coupled to the new architectures of the brains meant to understand them and fabricate them as products of the imagination. This process I refer to as Neurobiopolitics and the condition of this set of contingencies, Neuropower. When memory and attention are the focus of sovereignty's desire to administer the mindedness of its subjects the term Noo-politics as described by Maurizio Lazarrato is pertinent. As a result of the continuing development and sophistication of global media apparatti Noo-politics has given way to Neuropower. Neuropower concerns the production of the future man or woman through direct action on the subjects' Neuroplasticity. Neuropower produces Earthling as a new Global Subject in the production of the People of the Planet Earth possible. But there is another story. Like Biopower as described by Tony Negri and Michael Hardt in their book <u>Empire</u>, Neuropower has two sides. Neuropower is about administration but it is also about creation. In their most Utopian sense Artists, Architects, Designers, Writers, and Cinematographers, just to name a few, utilize there own methods, apparatti, histories, spaces, performances to produce another distribution of the sensible, a Redistribution of the Sensible, that competes with that of the aforementioned

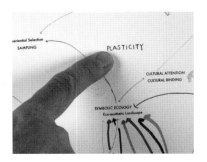

Fig. 6

Institutional Conditions for the attentions, memories and now neuroplasticity of the multitude. This is the real story of the Earthling drawing. Art Power! Art can be a form of Resistance in which the form(s) of the Distributed Sensibility is the conceptual palate through which new forms of imagination with their potential for difference are transfigured.

Fig. 7

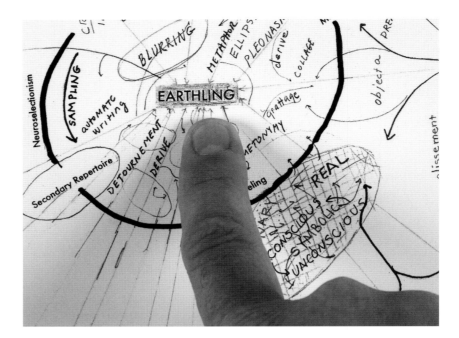

The diffuse logic of my now unconscious finger searching for the intense psychogeographic spaces finds itself, through diagonal and lingering gestures, in the cyclic looping Earthling Drawing. Here is where the dynamis of subjectivity is produced. Where the pre-indivuals of the singularities reside. Embedded in a spinning vortex of energy relations are histories of forms of that resistance to institutional norms which constitute the homogeneity of the people. Practices like The Paranoid Critical Method of Dali, the channeling and Theater of Cruelty of Artaud, the Ready-made of Duchamp, the Derive of Debord, the collage of John Heartfield, the automatic writing of Breton, which produce new objects, object relations, space, reactions and virtuoso performances. To these practices could be added the Race, Gender and Class Based practices that have become critically important in the past forty years. Here the work of Mary Kelly, Andrea Fraser, Felix Gonzales-Torres, Fred Wilson and Valie Export come to mind. These new conditions of the distribution of sensibility now populated by these other objects emanating from quite different conditions cause perturbations in the adjustment of the mind's eye as it scans the visual, auditory and haptic landscape in its daily routines. Through the same process of Neural Selectionism and its affect on the primary repertoire new connections are built. An "Other" Cultured Brain. As such attention and memory, the building blocks of the conscious and unconscious, are undeniably affected as well. As the world of imagination and fantasy create the internally mediated stimulation of those and other circuits neural sculpting and the mind will, though various feed-forward and feed back looping, be affected. Sovereignty in the age of controlling the mind at a distance is

hip to the contingencies of the possibility of culture as its competitor. The new war on culture and the differences it produces is taking many forms. From the reduction of funding, to the extended power of the market place, to the new interest in the funding of the what are referred to as the cultured industries, Sovereignty is doing all it can to usurp the power of the artist.

My finger stays here caught in the whirlpool of my endless fast forward thoughts. After lingering there for what seems like an eternity it slides out of this vortex upon the finely drawn mesh that creates the most superficial structure of the drawings, mimicking in some ways the field of electromagnetic rays produced by the sun that shower across the solar system. My finger follows a path of least resistance jumping from the primary repertoire into a directional flow past intraglobal mapping, interglobal mapping, cultural attention and the secondary repertoire, before finally alighting on the General Intellect. The General Intellect is positioned half way between the

Fig. 8

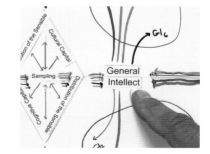

Primary/Secondary Repertoire Assemblage to it's right and a system of sampling mechanisms called Cultural Capitalism/ Cognitive Capitalism Assemblage on its left. It is continually in flux and is being formed simultaneously from the combined action

of these two Assemblages. My finger moves first to the left and crosses the perimeter of the diamond shaped platform. This platform is positioned at a crossroads formed by the horizontal flow mentioned above and a vertical productive flow above and below it. Through a process referred to here as sampling, two forms of political registry are formed. When the sampling process is co-joined to the apparatus of Cognitive Capital it creates a downward trend, which is at the service of sovereignty, producing the unified consciousness of a people. Cognitive Capital is usually referred to as the system of capital that generates and is generated by the conditions of a network society, in which the commodified digital products like the internet and computer games are components. A more extended definition would take into account immaterial labor that produces informational and cultural content as a commodity. As Maurizio Lazzarato has pointed out it refers to two different aspects of labor. First, it relates to that direct labor which involves skills related to cybernetics and and computer control. Second, it is defined by a set of activities not normally considered work such as the kind of communication involved in fixing artistic standards, fashions, tastes and consumer norms. Recently cognitive capitalism has expanded to include the commodification of what are referred to as externalities. One can think of this like the economist Yann Boutang: as an iceberg in which the top is labeled brand equity and the unseen underwater section it's externalites. Brand equity refers to the marketing effects or outcomes of a particular product because of its brand, as opposed to what its values and effects would be without it. Two kinds of dishwasher soap made out of the same materials are responded to quite differently because of their brand name and, as we will see, its brand allegiances, ie other brands to which it is associated and the network of symbolic capital it generates through communicative networks like gossip. These externalities, which in our iceberg model are beneath the water, are sometimes much larger then the brand equity we can actually see floating above. Like in the interpretation of dreams the brand equity might be looked at as the manifest content and the externalities its latent content. We have come to appreciate the effect that latent content can have in the interpretation of the meaning of the dream carried out as it sometimes is in and through talk therapy. Cognitive Capitalism has reached into the depths of that water to quantify and commodify, to give economic value to, these unseen factors. They factor into the spread-

sheet of investment and profit algorithms and are included in the projection of the effect that a specific marketing tool or procedure might have in the future. The intensive networks that make up the externalities are many times more complex and expansive then the brand equity itself, spreading its indirect effect into very diverse other networks that may have only rudimentary connection to the brand equity. Sometime ordered and sometime stochastic, these unseen networks can affect other groups who learn about the product indirectly as a result of communicative networks which occur far away from the target group but through long and tangential patterns roaming can find themselves directly affecting the prime stimulus. Their pre determination, production and commodification as real, form the new horizon of cognitive capitalism.

Cognitive capitalism takes on another role in this diagram that sets it off from Cultural Capitalism to be described shortly. In this drawing Cognitive Capitalism is a strategy of sampling. In an information society, characterized by immaterial labor defined anew in its political-ness as virtuoso performance, Cognitive Captialism and Cultural Captialism are two ways in which the information common is sampled to produce two very different types of General Intelligence. The info-Common is constantly evolving and expanding as ad infinitum condition. The common therefore is simultaneously ontogenic and epochal. On the one hand it is defined by the social, political, historical, economic, psychological and spiritual conditions it interfaces with. The internet is a kind of epochal common in this sense. We also know that the idea of the common was an idea generated during feudalism as a space that all who did not own land could use freely, which in later times was divided up between the new bourgoise who purchased it. Each common has a history of what it means to a particular culture. The conditions of the culture affect, as we will see later, the way in which it might be sampled.

In a Bergsonian way one can think of the common as constantly enlarging like the universe after the big bang. Darwinian approaches, in which ideas within specific symbolic niches are in competition with each other often, result in their subtraction from the market place of ideas. Such ideas are deemed lacking usefulness and are subtracted from the general repository of ideas, the Info-Common. In a Bergsonian Paradigm ideas are never lost but maintain themselves at varying levels of resonance awaiting a future cultural context and ecologic framework in which to reemerge. The common in this Bergsonian Model is constantly changing and expanding. Think of new music. DJ sampling has had the effect of expanding the potential of the music archive through its cutting and collaging strategies. Music compositions can be reworked and redeveloped to produce a completely new sound. The work of John Cage in the nineteen fifties expanded the idea of what could be used as a musical instrument to produce sound, for instance using a stone falling down a metal stair case, and what could be considered a usable and appreciated sound changing, for instance, the definition of noise and duration in music. Later Nam June Paik would take this a step further with his actual deconstruction of pianos to produce new forms of composition. Global Music has also expanded the global sonic archive as we in the western world become more and more familiar with the thousands of compositions from Mali, Ghana and the Middle East with their rich musical histories. But the internet itself is also expanding and until recently has provided another example of a immaterial and informational common which is constantly expanding with new content.

How this common is sampled marks the distinction between Cognitive Capital and Cultural Capital. Cognitive Capital is on the jurisdiction of the Institutional Understanding and samples the common in conjunction with its needs and aims. It is linked up to a specific Distribution of Sensibility, one which is defined by a distribution of that which can be commodified. The landscape of the real is one in which all things are labeled according to economic value. This Distribution of the Sensible, as it links up with Cognitive Capital, produces a system of self-evident facts that are distributed throughout the experiential landscape where they compete with those produced by the Cultural Capital/ Redistribution dyad. Together they produce a set of perceptual and affectual contingencies which determines what is visible and audible as well as what can be said, thought, made or done. Strictly speaking, distribution therefore refers both to forms of inclusion and to forms of exclusion.

Cultural Captial as it functions in this diagram is somewhat different than how it functions in the universe of Pierre Bordieu. He creates two forms of capital that are important for the field of cultural production. First is Symbolic Capital which refers to the degree of accumulated prestige, celebrity, and honor. Secondly is Cultural

Capital which he develops most fully in his book Distinction and which relates to what he refers to as cultural competency, the ability to decipher the secret codes and knowledge subsumed in aesthetic artifacts like paintings. The possession of this code is Cultural Capital and it is acquired through a long process of acquisition either through the agency of the family, working artists or in the art academy. In this diagram Cultural Capital is also related to the understanding of this code. But here Cultural Capital leads to Art Power. Cognitive Capital, as it is in competition with Cultural Capital, constantly attempts to undermine its crucial role and its power. Through processes like Alternative Institutionalization, ideas and works produced by the desire for difference are homogenized. In the cultural sphere they are reenacted in the context of a capitalized universe to become a kind of revolutionary generator for Cognitive Capitalism, which is always looking for new ideas to appropriate. Janis Joplin's song of rebellion, itself an appropriation of Mississippi Delta Blues, "Oh Lord Won't You Buy Me a Mercedes Benz", now embellishes a Mercedes Benz commercial. Cognitive Capitalism as a means to administer memory and attention utilizes the conditions of nostalgic remembering in a subset of the population with buying power i.e. baby boomers who took part in 1960s alternative culture, to induce the desire to buy a Mercedes Benz. Cultural Capital here is a means of sampling the ever expanding common in a very different way then Cognitive Capitalism to generate an alternative distribution of the sensible, a Redistribution of the Sensible. Artists using their own methods, apparatti, processes, materials, histories and organizational and social networks produce alternative products that populate the cultural environment, calling out through a different form of attention another pluripotentiality of the brain in the inscribing upon its network facilities a different organizational disposition, in the end leading to the potential for new forms of thought and creativity. This is the other side of what I am calling Neuropower. On the one hand the Institutional Understanding through the dispositif of Cognitive Capital and The Distribution of the Sensible creating the atomic sameness and homogeny of the administered and extensive people and on the other hand, Cultural Capitalism and the Redistribition of the Sensible creating the monadic difference and heterogeneity of the un-administered multitude.

Berlin, 2008.

Drawings   2004 - 2008

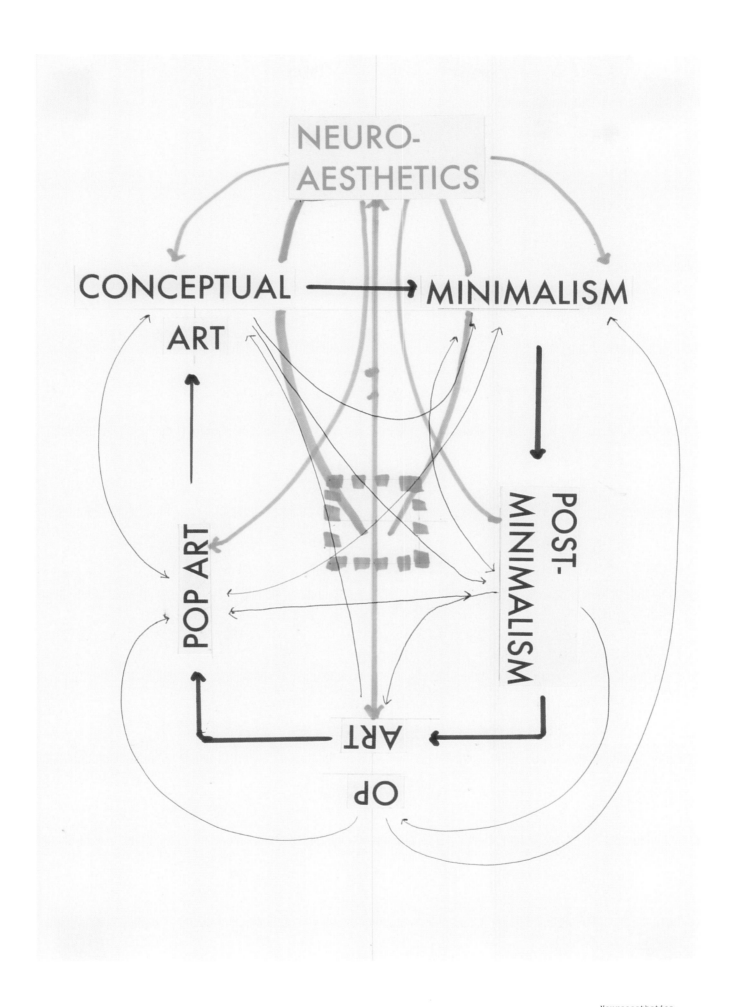

Neuroaesthetics,
2006, graphite and magic marker on
paper, 29.5 x 41.8cm.

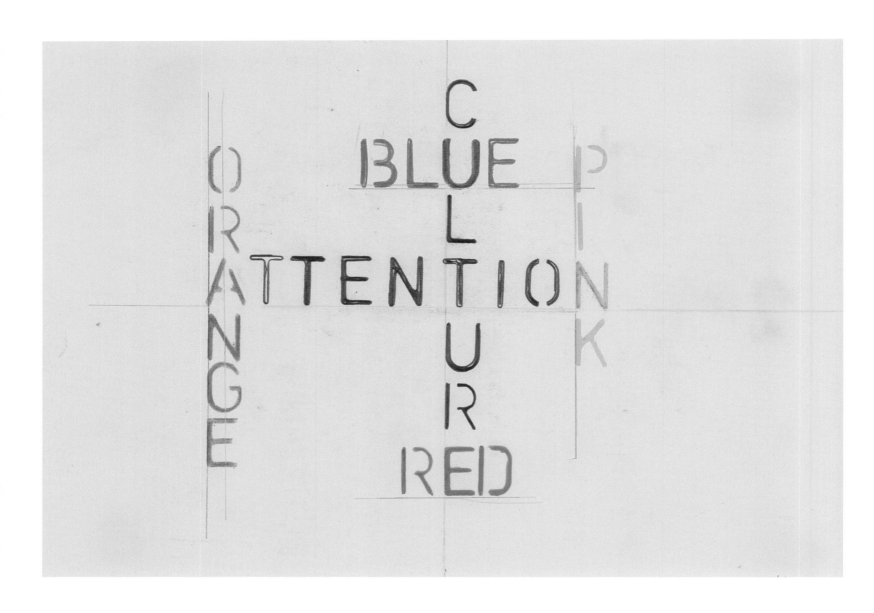

Attention,
2005, colored pencil and graphite on
paper, 29.7 x 21 cm.

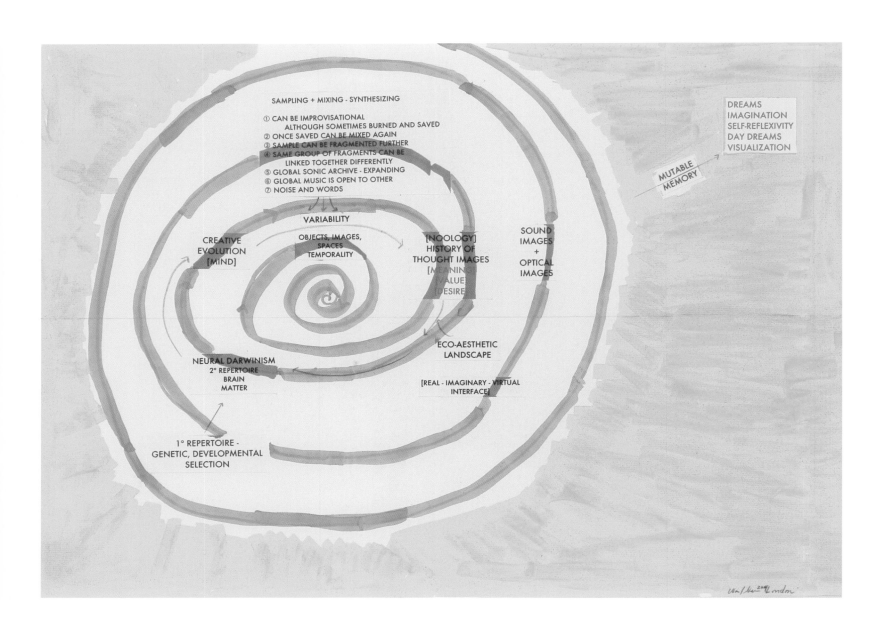

SAMPLING + MIXING - SYNTHESIZING

① CAN BE IMPROVISATIONAL
   ALTHOUGH SOMETIMES BURNED AND SAVED
② ONCE SAVED CAN BE MIXED AGAIN
③ SAMPLE CAN BE FRAGMENTED FURTHER
④ SAME GROUP OF FRAGMENTS CAN BE
   LINKED TOGETHER DIFFERENTLY
⑤ GLOBAL SONIC ARCHIVE - EXPANDING
⑥ GLOBAL MUSIC IS OPEN TO OTHER
⑦ NOISE AND WORDS

VARIABILITY

OBJECTS, IMAGES,
SPACES
TEMPORALITY

CREATIVE
EVOLUTION
[MIND]

[NOOLOGY]
HISTORY OF
THOUGHT IMAGES
[MEANING]
VALUE]
[DESIRE]

SOUND
IMAGES
+
OPTICAL
IMAGES

DREAMS
IMAGINATION
SELF-REFLEXIVITY
DAY DREAMS
VISUALIZATION

MUTABLE
MEMORY

ECO-AESTHETIC
LANDSCAPE

NEURAL DARWINISM
2° REPERTOIRE
BRAIN
MATTER

[REAL - IMAGINARY - VIRTUAL
INTERFACE]

1° REPERTOIRE -
GENETIC, DEVELOPMENTAL
SELECTION

Sampling the Light Fantastic,
2005, magic marker on paper,
41.8 x 29.5cm.

80

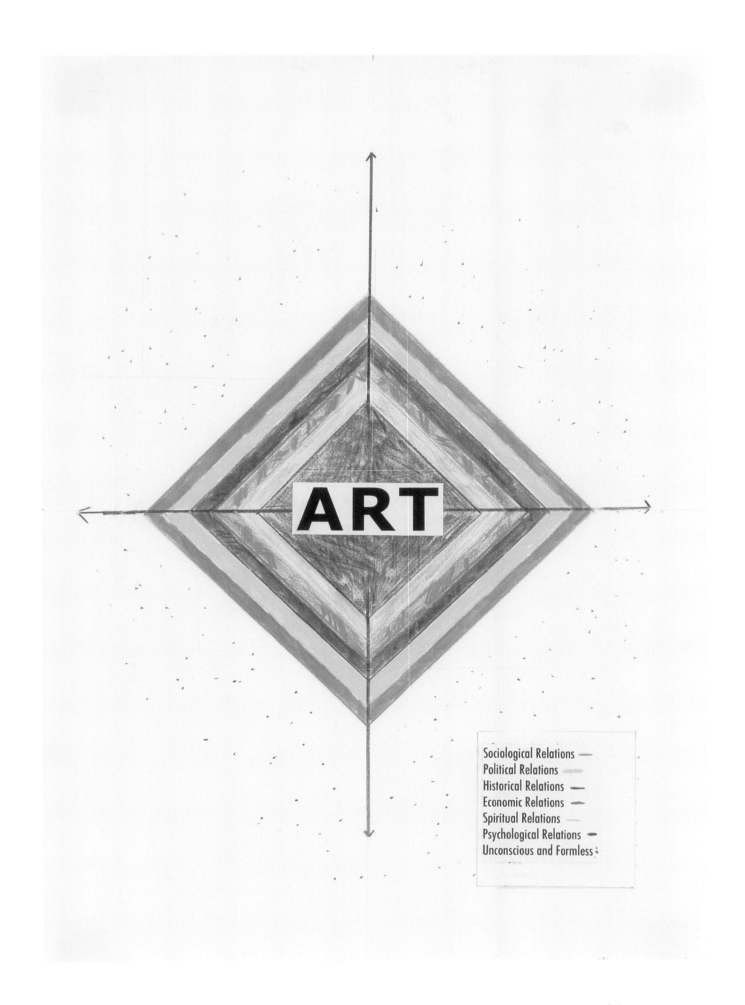

Sociological Relations —
Political Relations —
Historical Relations —
Economic Relations —
Spiritual Relations —
Psychological Relations —
Unconscious and Formless

Art,
2005, magic marker, graphite, colored pencil on paper, 29.5 x 41.8cm

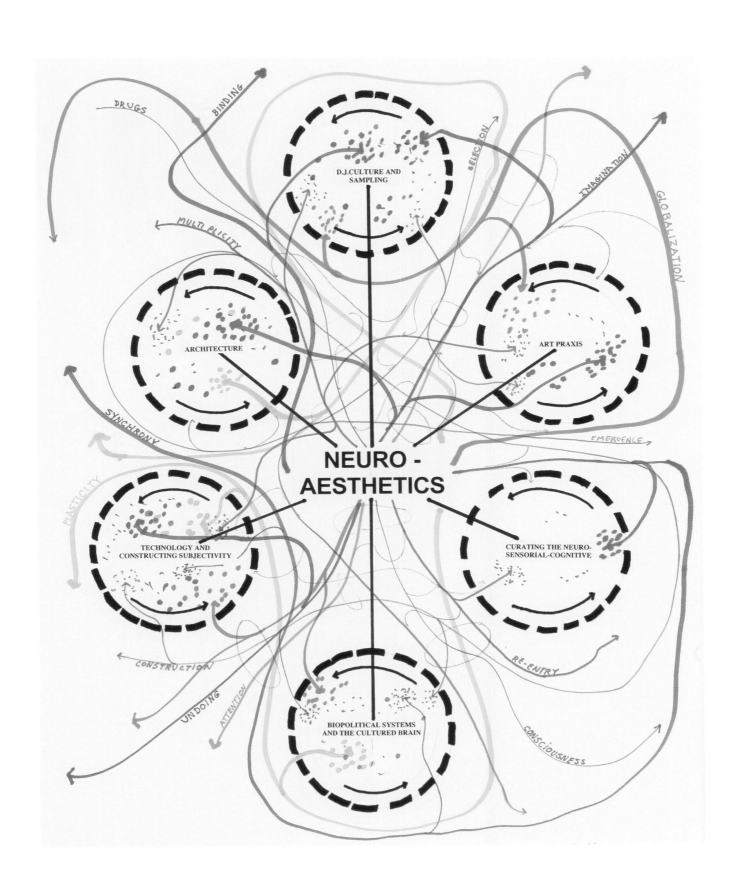

Drawing for Neuroaesthetics
Conference, 2005, graphite, magic
marker on paper, 45.6 x 56.7cm.

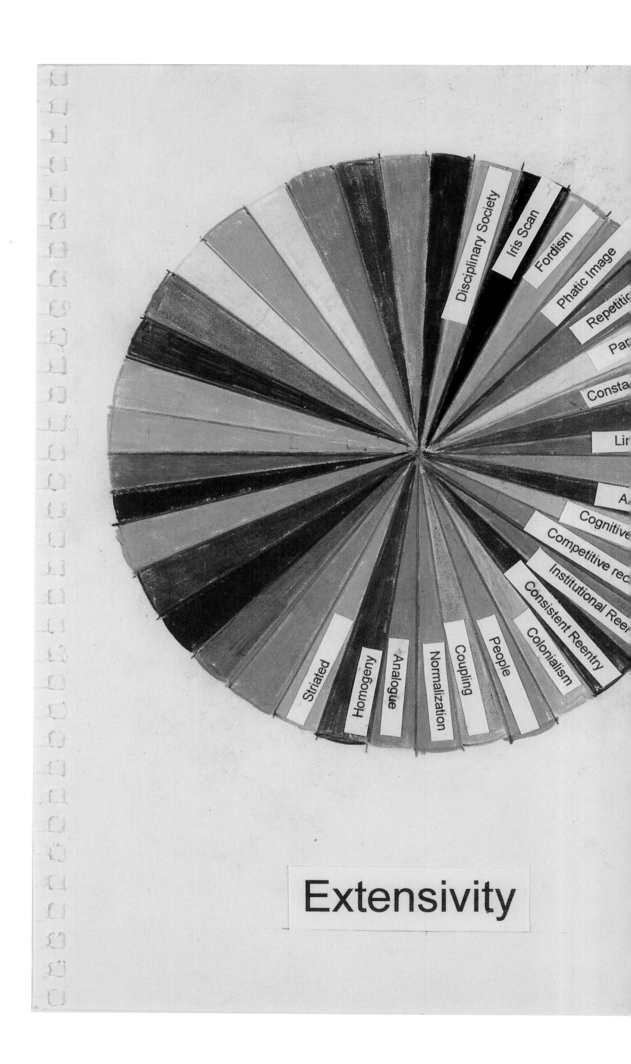

Disciplinary Society
Iris Scan
Fordism
Phatic Image
Repetiti
Par
Consta
Lir
A
Cognitive
Competitive re
Institutional Reer
Consistent Reentry
Colonialism
People
Coupling
Normalization
Analogue
Homogeny
Striated

Extensivity

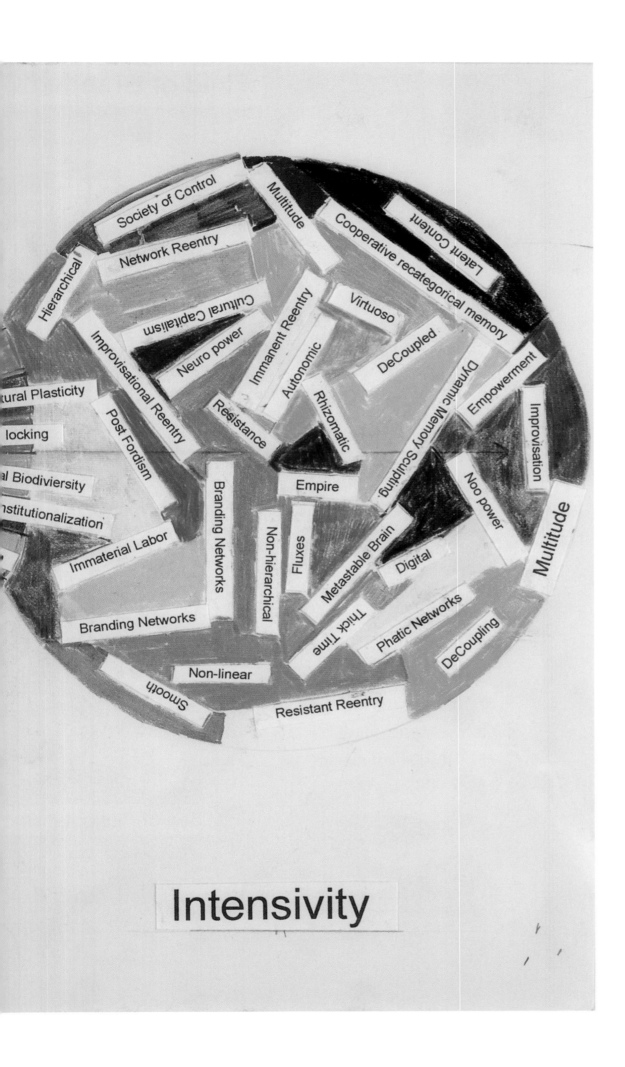

Intensivity

Lost between the Extensivity /
Intensivity Exchange, 2008,
colored pencil on paper,
35.5 x 28cm.

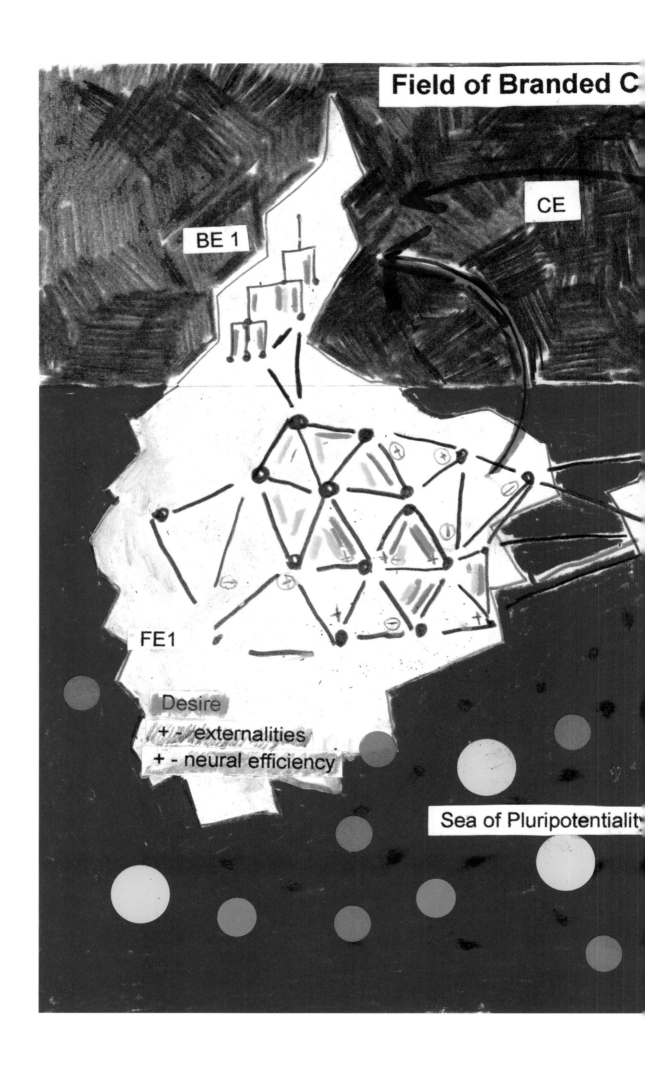

Field of Branded Contingencies, 2008, colored pencil, graphite, magic marker, colored stickers on paper, 26.1 x 20cm.

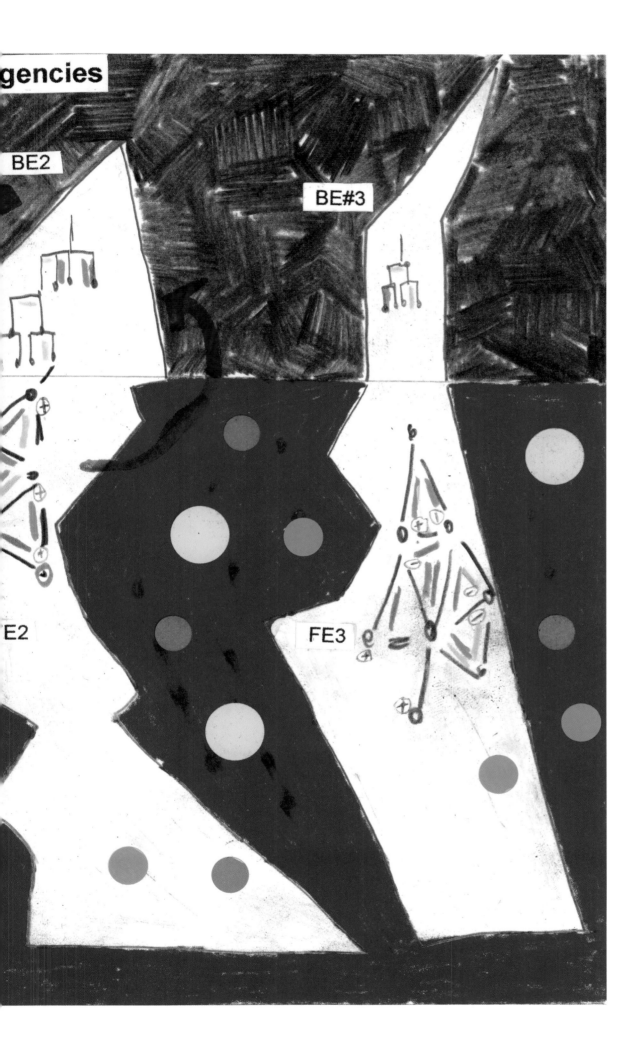

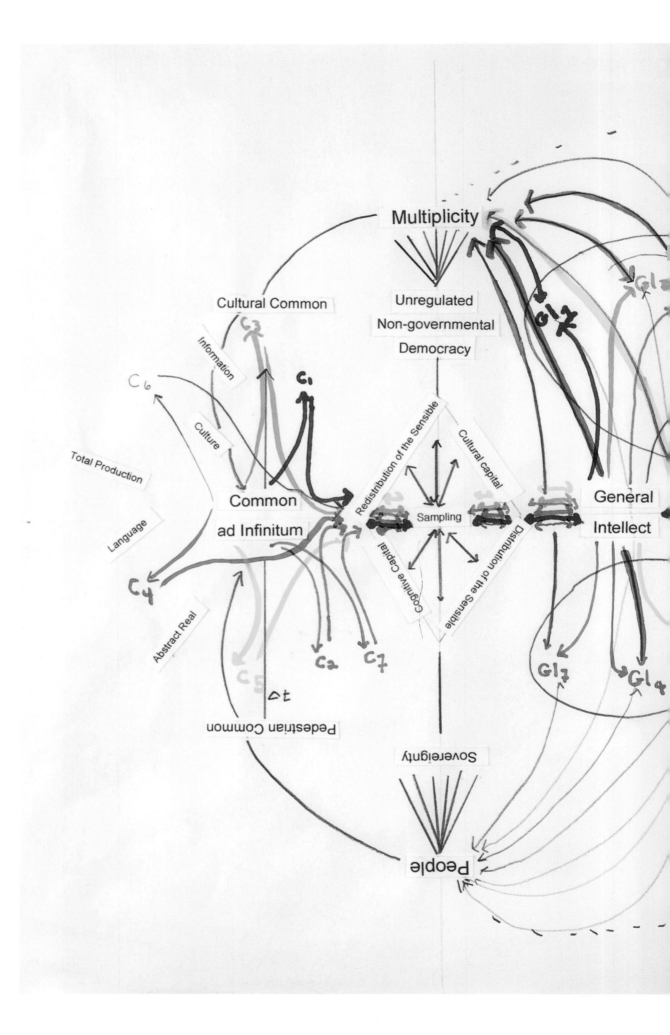

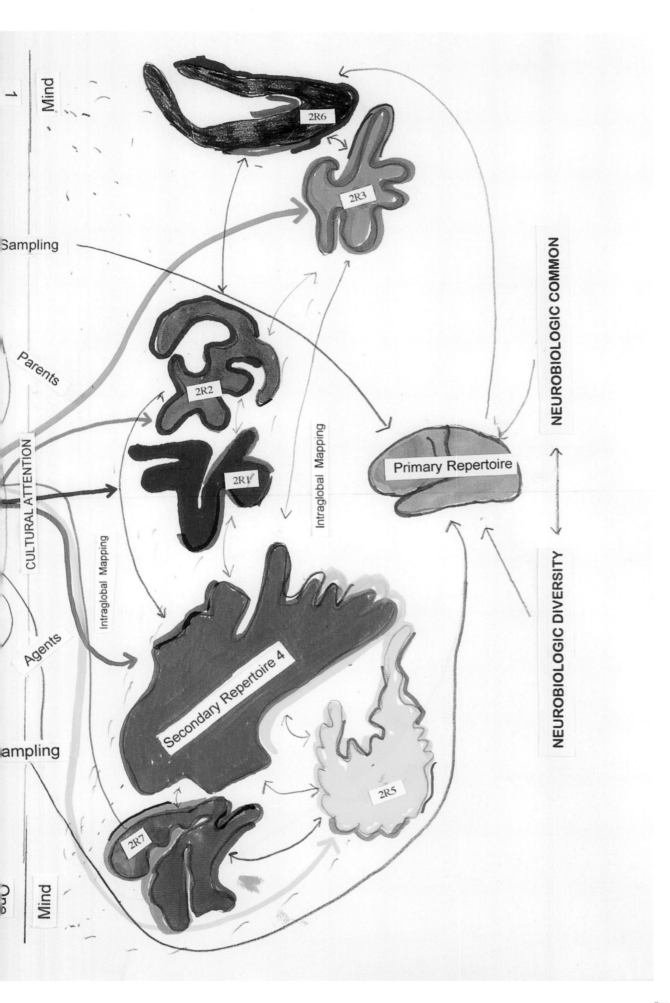

89

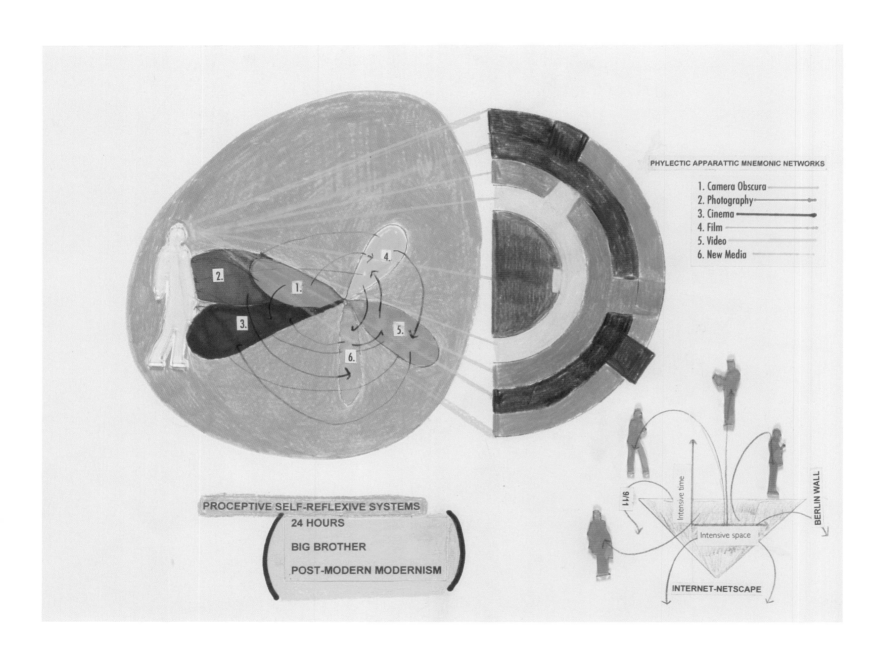

PHYLECTIC APPARATTIC MNEMONIC NETWORKS

1. Camera Obscura
2. Photography
3. Cinema
4. Film
5. Video
6. New Media

PROCEPTIVE SELF-REFLEXIVE SYSTEMS

24 HOURS

BIG BROTHER

POST-MODERN MODERNISM

Intensive time

Intensive space

1/1/6

BERLIN WALL

INTERNET-NETSCAPE

Proceptive Self-Reflexive System,
2006, colored pencil, magic marker
and graphite on paper,
39.7 x 29.8 cm.

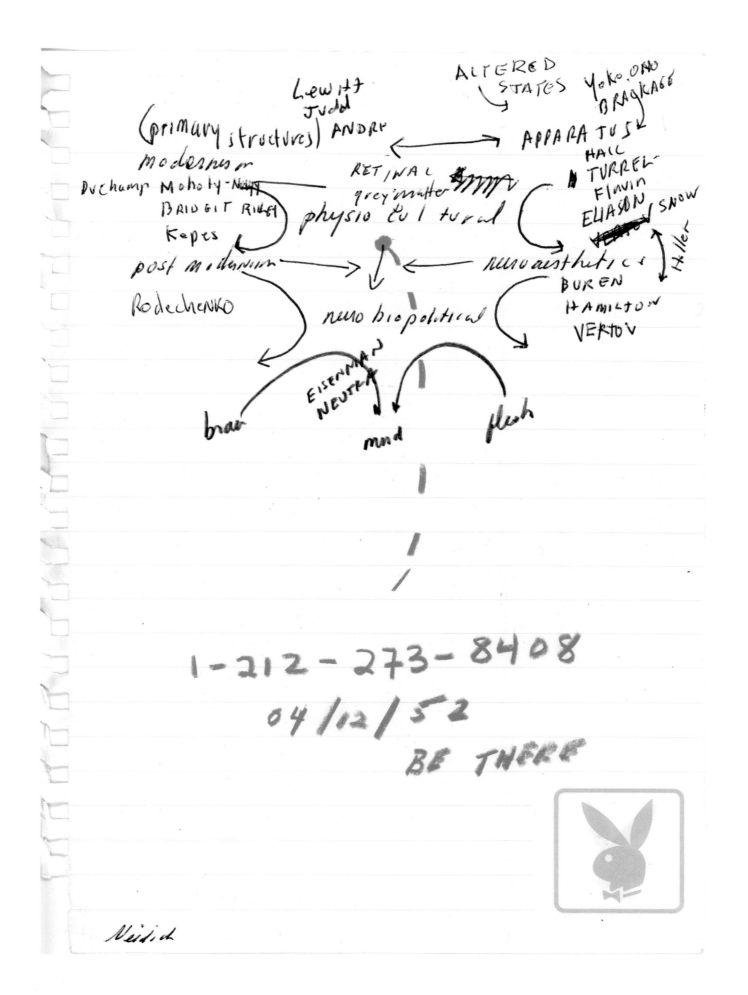

Grey Matters,
2008, colored pencil, graphite
and ink pen on paper, 15 x 21cm.

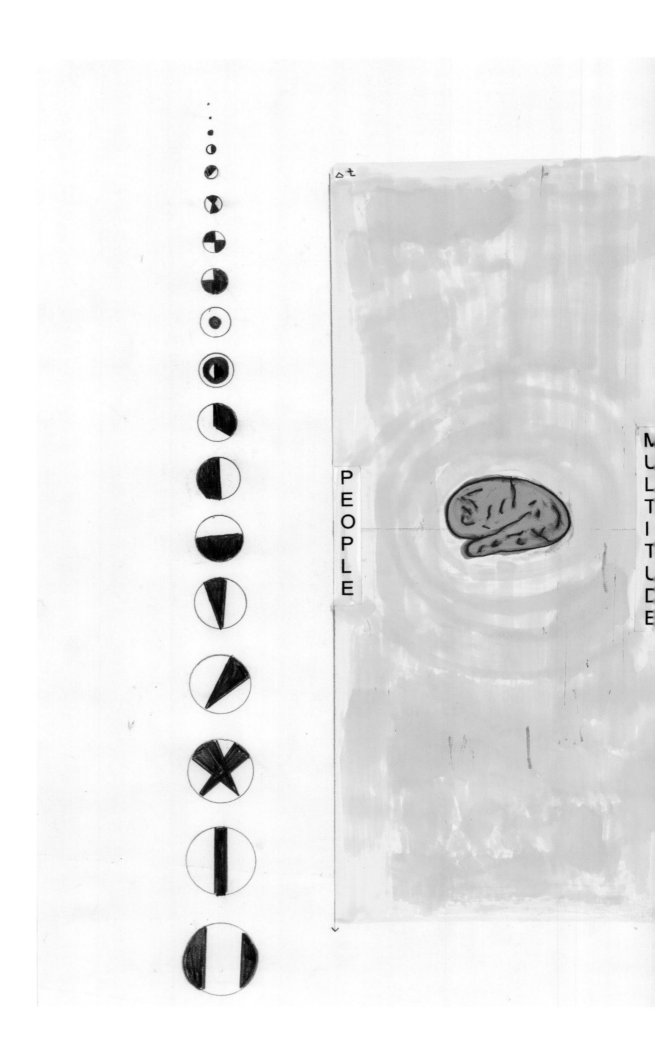

Suprematism

Conceptual Art

Surrealism

Abstract Expressionism

Dada

Cubism

Shaping the Negation of
the Negation, 2008, graphite,
magic marker, on paper,
56.9 x 46.1cm.

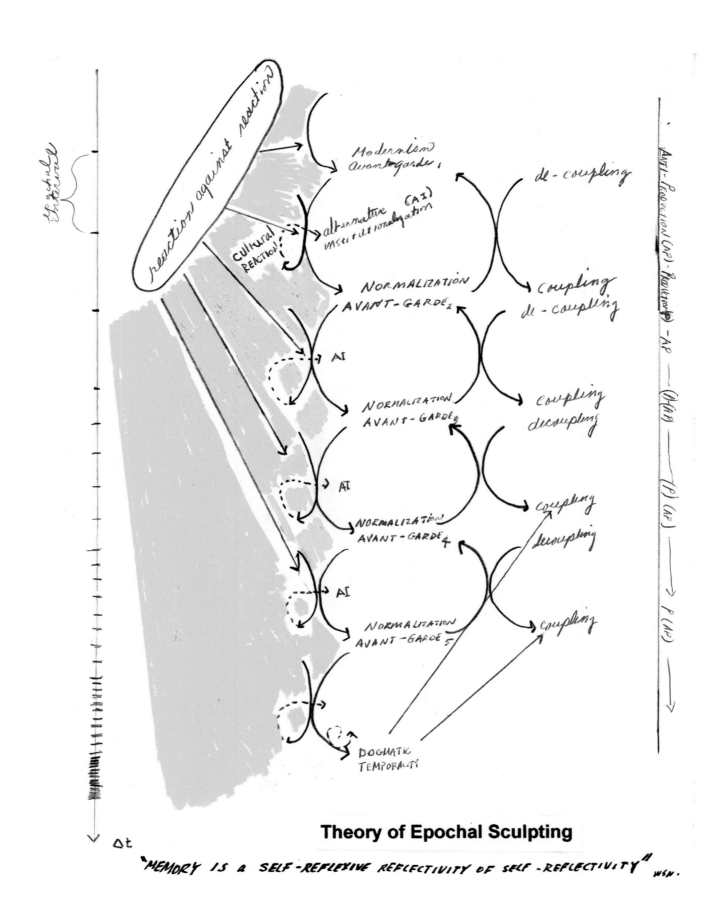

Theory of Epochal Sculpting

"MEMORY IS A SELF-REFLEXIVE REFLECTIVITY OF SELF-REFLECTIVITY" WSN.

Theory of Epochal Sculpting, 2008,
colored pencil, graphite, ink pen
on paper, 20 x 26.1cm.

94

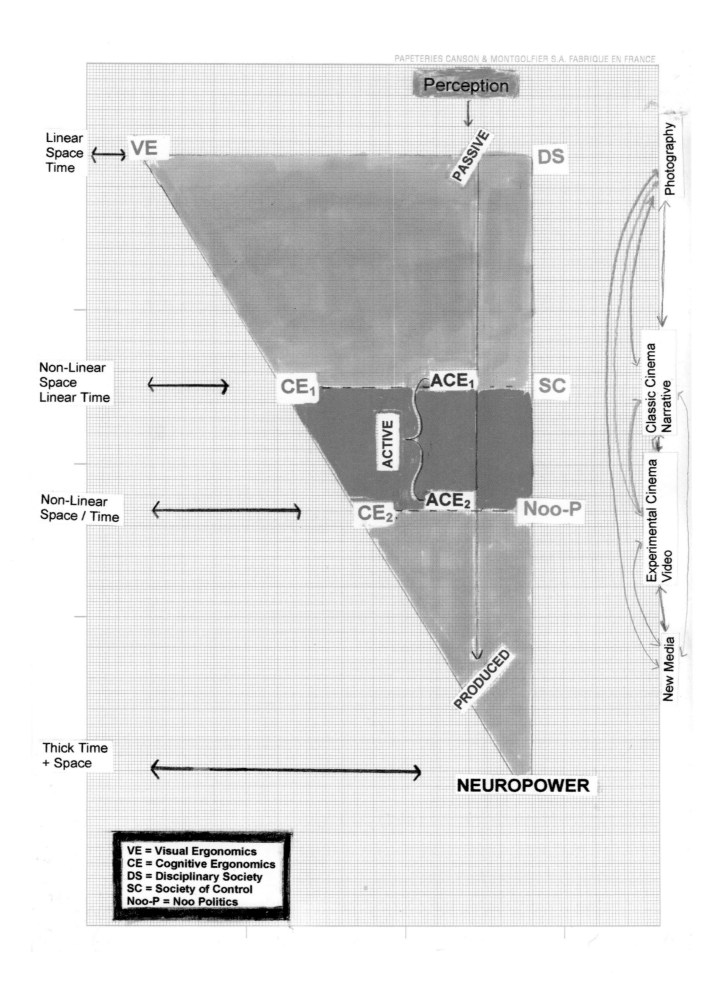

Neuropower, 2008, colored pencil, graphite, magic marker on paper, 21 x 29.6cm.

95

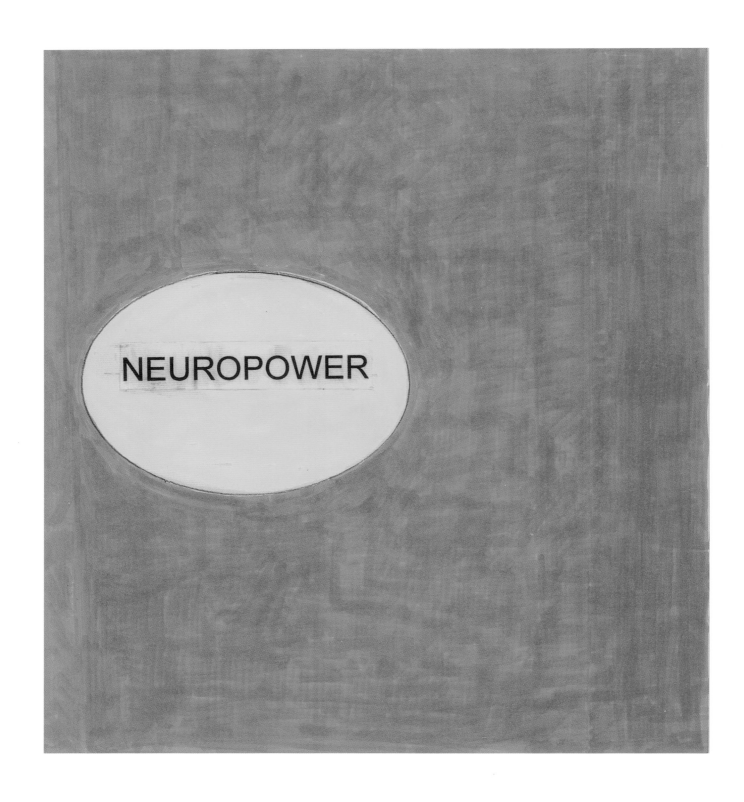

Neuropower,
2008, magic marker on paper,
25.4 x 27.9cm.

Lost Between the Extensivity / Intensivity Exchange

Onomatopee, Eindhoven, The Netherlands, 2008

Get a Grip

Freek Lomme

I cannot wander through Warren Neidich's solo exhibition 'Lost Between the Extensivity / Intensivity Exchange' at Onomatopee as the visitor I usually am when I intend to review an exhibition. When I review an exhibition I face visual material in a chronological way, starting behind the entrance, through a passage, often a reception room, and further on into the deep of the exhibition space. I like to end these visits walking back to the reception room to pick up the hall text, sometimes accompanied by a small oral exchange with the person in charge of the reception desk.

However, in reality, I am currently residing behind the reception desk, my desk as director/curator of Onomatopee, working on a text about the exhibition. Therefore, dear reader, you will understand that my engagement with this exhibition is as a non-visitor and as a witness to a different kind of chronology. I was, evidently, present when the exhibition came into being. For me the coherence between the numerous objects within this show, resulting in a careful assemblage of visual data, manifested in a specific order of production. The coherence I envision is not the one present, the end result, with its current spatial arrangement and architectural display, but rather one that evolved in the course of its production, being the logical result of the efforts we made as a team during its installation. Therefore I cannot review this exhibition as an outsider and would like to write on the exhibition from the perspective of the curator.

Poetical engagement and hope.
I first saw the work of Warren Neidich as a visitor of the exhibition Multitasking at the Stedelijk Museum 's-Hertogenbosch (SM's), in which a series of very colorful diagrams were displayed upon a long white shelf attached to the wall at waist height. My strong reaction at this initial encounter was triggered by the strange combination of signifiers: words, symbols, sketches, references and all kind of sources that seemed to signify something. I encountered a quest, a brainstorm. Still, it suggested way more than that. The works did not just entail simply a group of signifiers caught in various intersecting flows, they also registered on a grander scale. As such, the drawings

proposed that to be true to yourself, two seemingly opposing views needed to be reconciled. First, that a relation to the world is both a playful thing, wherein we never lose the innocent eagerness of an exploring child with no limits and, at the same time, the more serious business of respecting knowledge and the cultural memory that retains it. To learn true and to truly exist, means to both respect and to incorporate knowledge into your daily play of signifying.

This kind of work visually engages as it analytically challenges. Since I consider good art to have the quality, in the words of Dutch philosopher Rob van Gerwen, to challenge both experience and knowledge, this work did suffice. Even more so, good art must surpass the issue of artistic autonomy. Simultaneously it should respect subjective dispositions; the viewer is challenged to engage with the work on his or her own terms within this public arena. The work of Warren Neidich respected imagination as an analytic quality within a totality of utter poetry, leaving enough space for the visitor's subjective formation of social-psychological mapping. In respect to visual culture this criticality is crucial and essential. This is an attribute that Onomatopee, as a practice, as publisher and presentation space, endeavors to make manifest.

Poetical witnessing and production assistance.
When we met at Onomatopee for the second time, Warren was working with the idea of simply projecting his drawing pieces, his diagrams, generated on the walls of his IASPIS Residency in Stockholm, Sweden, upon our walls, ceiling and floor. As many Situationist paradigms inspire his working methods, this detournement of his mind map upon an alternative set of architectural conditions seemed very exciting. When reviewing the space a few months before the installation, he noticed some pedestals, architectural symbols of the white cube's display facility and immediately envisioned his projections upon them: a projection of a convoluted and folded mind analogue onto the mathematically derived secure basis for absolute modernism represented by the geometric pedestal. Such a projection would become even more fragile and immanent if the pedestals could move around on dollies, like one he saw out of the corner of his

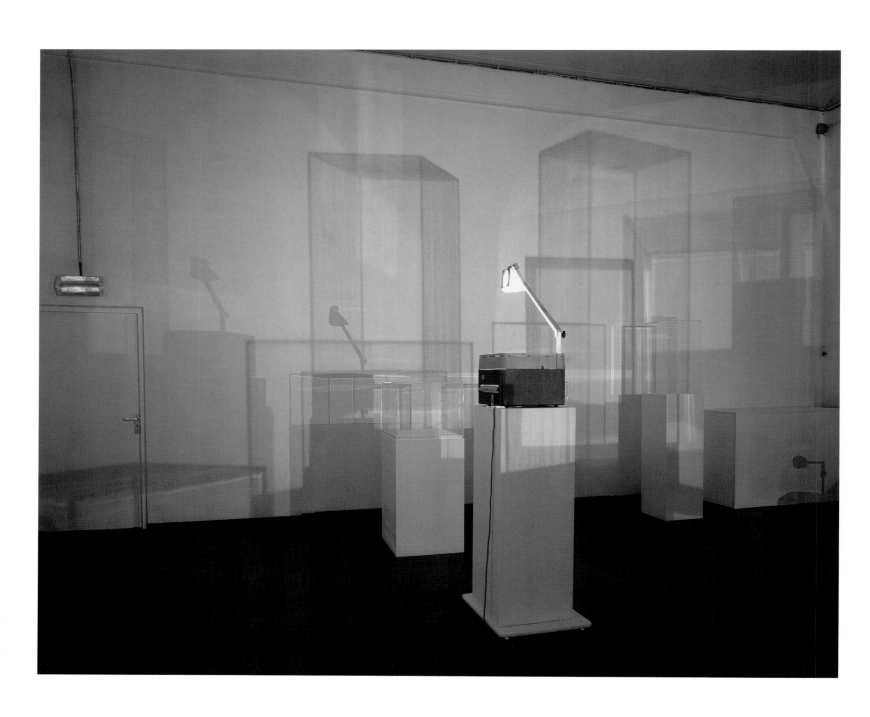

eye resting quietly in a corner of the space. Later on he envisioned Plexiglas cubes fitted to the pedestals, which acted as large lenses whereby he could generate beautiful shadowy projections upon the walls of the white cube. This worked well on a symbolic level since it elegantly displayed the underbelly of modernism: its roots in the unconscious and the notion of the architectural uncanny. I was a witness to both its symbolic and spatial becoming. These two were in a continuous, overall exchange.

Later on I received an e-mail, stating that he wanted to add his Neuroaesthetic Library to that of a collection of books in the Public Library in Eindhoven. His idea was to insinuate his private collection into a public one. Each book would be designated with a Dewey Decimal Classification number and be mixed in the shelves with the public collection designated with a red rather than customary black number. These books, together with an accompanying poster displaying the key to its symbols, would produce a nested field of knowledge within the larger one contextualized by the library and could bring the usages of analytic resources to the mind map of ordinary people as well as refer to the exhibition at Onomatopee. We tried the public library, but they considered it too difficult to gain all the books; the library of the Van Abbemuseum liked the idea but was programmed already. To worsen things, Warren hurt his back carrying a package of books through the London Underground and therefore did not want to move the books over himself in order to install them at Onomatopee. He consequently came up with the idea to present a bibliography instead and display it above the reception desk in our production office. Remco, my Onomatopee partner and graphic designer, designed four long scrolls that could be printed and ergonomically installed in the old-time fashion of maps on wooden dowels that adorned so many of our school halls. Meanwhile, I received a call from Warren wherein he proposed that we should provide white painting overalls for the visitors to the gallery who would thereby become projection surfaces/screens as they moved inside the exhibition space, thus incorporating them into the exhibition architecture as symbolic components acting within the environmental mind map. The white overalls I found were too similar to the ones used in laboratories, so we continued to search, finally finding some everyday white shirts. Nudity would have been an option as well but in the end it seemed too distracting.

Of course a curator is not an artist and of course Warren is more specialized in his field than I. I soon became aware that Warren's practice entails an awful lot. He seems to have an idea projecting his paradigm upon all aspects of his work: architectural, theoretical, symbolical and so forth. Let's be clear: Warren's work never gained a pure theoretical compaction, serving as fallacy to his authority. Nevertheless, I do respect his authority and the subjects of authority he puts forth, since Warren respects the subjectivity of the viewer and leaves enough space, purposefully and with determined conviction, to engage with his work.

The resulting installation situated an environment wherein a creative mind could engage with the visual and textual information in a subject specific manner. Since this entire spectrum was still developing in a vibrant motion during the installation period, my task was to follow his enormous urge to connect various layers and objects and to rely on his capabilities and have faith in the artistic practice that would result. This text and book serve as the outcome, not just of the exhibition but also of his recent work; in a way this work could again be considered an ontological exercise, not in a dogmatic, autonomous way, but as a subject and site-specific endeavor, true to each cause, true to optional effects.

Assembled results

Can we, within space and time, comprehend our position or do we have to accept given circumstances? Do we function or does it function us? Do we have free will and how can we postulate that free will? These questions rose within my mind when working on Neidich's exhibition.

Can we fade and focus while we're physically bound within a socio-economic hierarchy that is ever present in the art world? Neidich managed to situate many dispositions on this behalf within one installation: three dimensional, two dimensional, social and abstract. The mental domain and the physical domain engage in a interactive manner, suiting both an associative as an analytical disposition. All these dispositions acted on the fracture of system and subjectivity through a physical embodiment. This is what made the exhibition very human friendly: the comprehensible architecture, its obvious symbolism as icons of bourgeois cultural capital, and our equally validated human embodiment within this setting. Everything caught up in aesthetics: system, represented by the projectors and pedestals; subject, represented by the projections and the dynamics of projected associative assemblage and the potency of movement on behalf of the pedestals; and the social, through equally validating the bodies of visitors, through the white shirts, with the pedestals and projectors. We exist within the embodiment of this situation. We live within the 'space of flows' and just have to relate to this.

Still, this is nothing new: a plurality of subjective viewpoints has always existed and the simultaneity of paradigms can be regarded quite common sense as well. What makes this work unique is the connection between the physical domain of subjects and the non-physical domain of various systems. We live within absolute constraints but have the liberty to add this up with our own intelligence: we can combine site-specifics with subject-specifics within reach of our own moral engagement. We are given the circumstances for this engagement in a self-respectful and social manner, through a contextual, spatial oriented intelligibility. Let's be clear: it's up to us!

We can take caring responsibility and are welcomed by Warren to get a grip through a subject- and site-specific stance. This grip does not close off from any theoretical, systematic and analytic stance but incorporates them into our physical and non-physical body of signification. This is important in regard to "popular cultures" and populisms' decaying respect of knowledge. The subject- and site-specific stance also notes that this decaying respect is a result of our individual lack to comprehend the system's politics as a whole. This is the key to understanding this exhibition. In the intensive logics that are predominate in this age of Neo-liberal Global Capitalism the nature of knowledge has changed as well. It is impossible for any one person to comprehend it all and we have difficulty determining where it begins or ends. We are not at the end of philosophy as so many have determined but the end of the sense of the dialectic. This requires new forms of understandings and new kinds of dispositifis, as Foucault would call them,[1] in order to engage with it; dispositifs yet to be invented or, if they have been not yet, incorporated into the larger and intensive machinic assemblages that are now necessary for understanding. We're finally getting to the stage of true emancipation, populism illustrates us the truth of this within an almost anomic situation. This also illustrates the urgency for a new formation of dispositifs, an individual oriented one, determined by our own moral stance. Neidich's installation on one hand draws attention to the complexity and incomprehensibility of this urgency for we are in between the logics as circumscribed and produced through a unified and quite absolute consciousness of a singular people and on the other hand draws on the logics of the reformative and individual creative potential, which attributes a multiplicity engaged with the back end of this system, since it seems so damn fragile and empty. As a faith fallen Catholic boy, I appreciate this and consider this stance of vital and respectful importance.

To be more explicit, I will conclude with foregrounding the resulting Aesthetic Library, as displayed beside our reception desk. This work, being integral to the installation as a whole, seems both to hand in, positively formulated, available resources for further negotiation and formation; as negatively formulated, a memorial to all fundamental modernist notions on the feasibility of our world. Let's be glad that our memory is damn vulnerable, that our memory is selective and can only make us pessimist when we lose motivation to engage with it. We're only 'Lost between the extensivity/intensivity exchange' to the extent we release our depressions.

Get a grip!

---

1. In Foucauld's disciplinary society power is being executed by a wide range of disciplinary machines (**dispositifs**), like schools, prisons, mental institutes and so forth. These institutes form the individual, produce the subject.

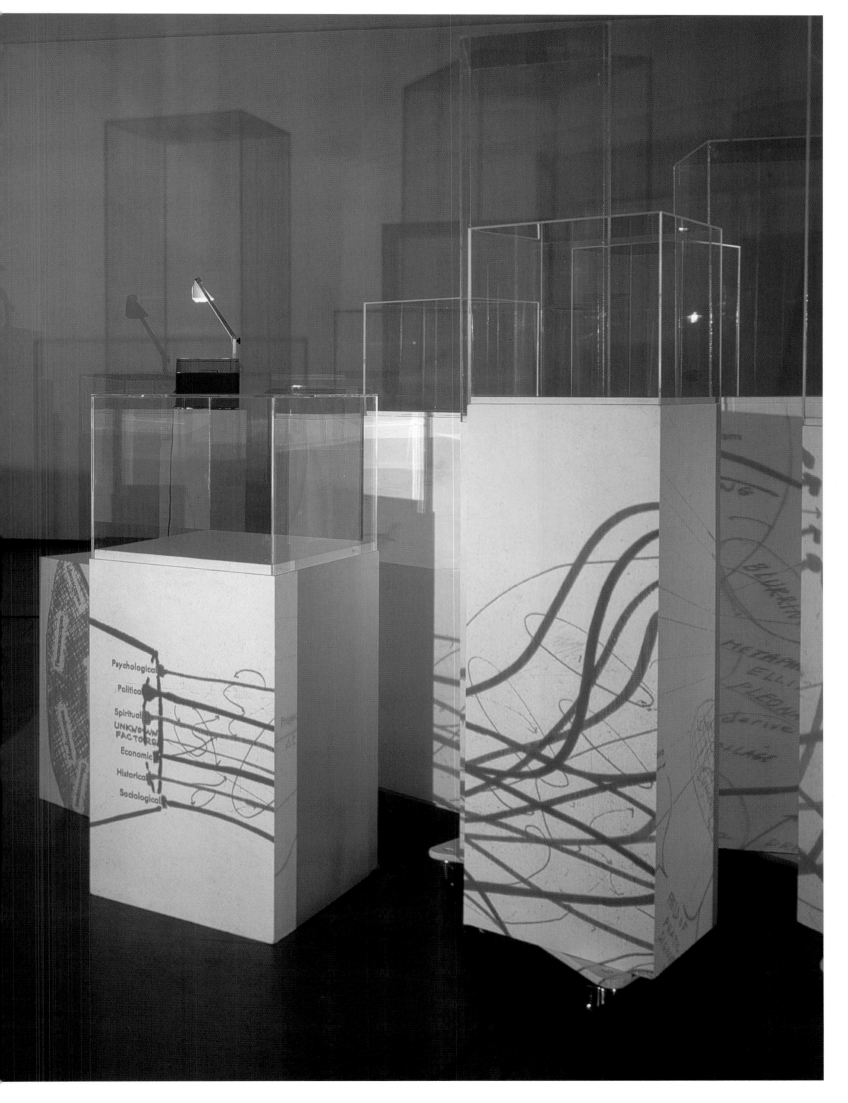

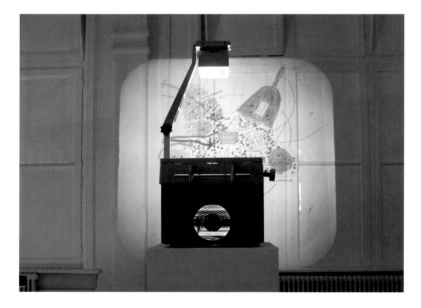

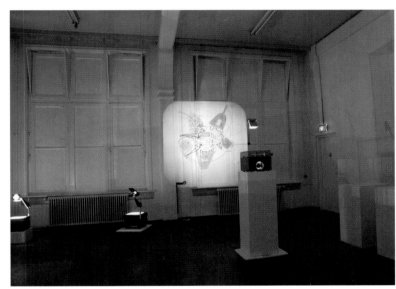
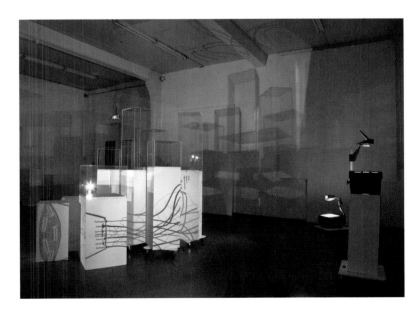

Lost Between the Extensivity /
Intensivity Exchange, 2008, mixed
media: painted wooden pedestals,
various sizes; plexiglass boxes,
variable sizes; transparencies;
overhead projectors; installation
views.

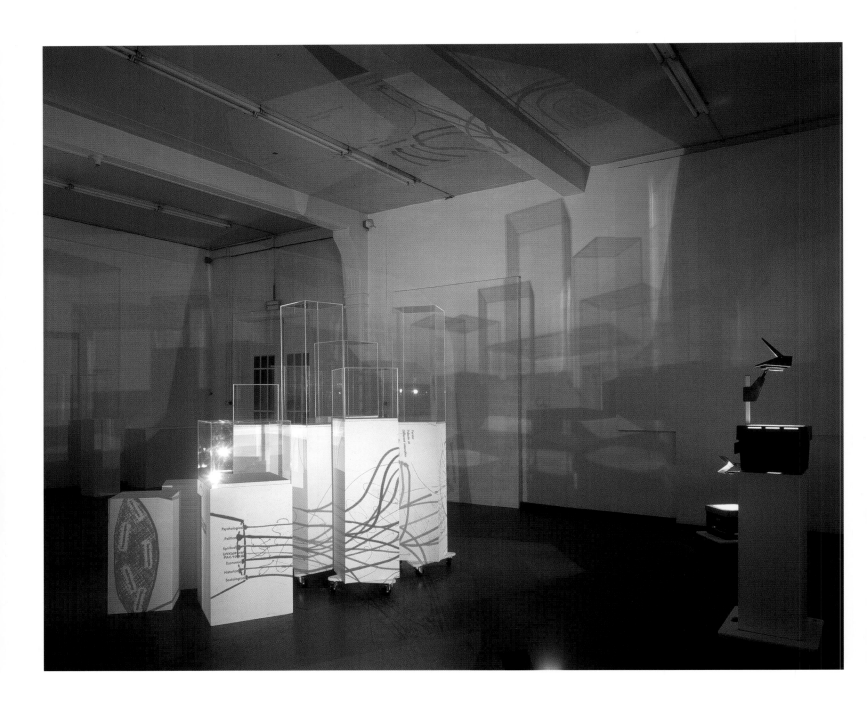

Lost Between the Extensivity /
Intensivity Exchange, 2008, mixed
media: painted wooden pedestals,
various sizes; plexiglass boxes,
variable sizes; transparencies;
overhead projectors; installation
views.

The Neuro-
Aesthetic Library

2004 - 2008

1. ABBOTT, EDWIN, **Flatland**, Princeton, Princeton University Press, 1991 **2.** ADORNO, THEODOR W., **Aesthetic Theory**, trans. Robert Hullot-Kentor, Minneapolis, University of Minnesota Press, 1997. **3.** ADORNO, THEODOR W., **Minima Moralia: Reflections on a Damaged Life**, London, Verso, 1991. **4.** ADORNO, THEODOR W., **The Culture Industry**, J.M. Bernstein, ed., London, Routledge Classics, 1991. **5.** ADORNO, THEODOR W., BENJAMIN, WALTER, BLOCH, ERNST, BRECHT, BERTOLD, LUKACS, GEORG, **Aesthetics and Politics. The Key Texts of the Classic Debate within German Marxism**, Afterword by Fredric Jameson, Ronald Taylor, trans. eds., London,Verso, sixth printing, 2002. **6.** ADORNO, THEODORE, W. AND HORKHEIMER, MAX, **Dialectic of Enlightenment**, New York, Herder and Herder, 1972. **7.** AGAMBEN, GIORGIO, **Homo Sacer: Sovereign Power and Bare Life**, Stanford, Stanford University Press, 1998. **8.** AGAMBEN, GIORGIO, **The Open: Man and Animal**, Stanford, Stanford University Press, 2004. **9.** ALISON, JANE, **Colour after Klein. Rethinking Colour in Modern and Contemporary Art**, Barbican Art Gallery, London, Black Dog Publishing, Exhibition Catalogue, 2007. **10.** ALLMAN, JOHN, **Evolving Brains**, New York, Scientific American Library, 1999. **11.** ALTHUSSER, LOUIS, **On Ideology**, London, New York, Verso, 2008. **12.** APPADURAI, ARJUN, **Modernity at Large: Cultural Dimensions of Globalization**, Minneapolis, University of Minnesota Press, 2000. **13.** AURELI, PIER VITTORIO, **The Project of Autonomy. Politics and Architecture within and against Capitalism**, Princeton NJ, coproduction of the Buell Center/Forum Project and Princeton Architectural Press, 2008. **14.** BACHELARD, GASTON, **The Poetics of Space**, Maria Jolas trans., Boston USA, Beacon Press, 1969. **15.** BARON-COHEN, SIMON, TAGER-FLUSBERG, HELEN, AND COHEN, DONALD J., EDS, **Understanding Other Minds. Perspectives From Development Cognitive Neuroscience**, Second Edition, Oxford University Press, USA, 2000. **16.** BASAR, EROL, **Memory and Brain dynamics: Oscillations Integrating Attention, Perception, Learning, and Memory**, Boca Raton, CRC Press, 2004. **17.** BATAILLE, GEORGES, **Eroticism, Death and Sensuality**, San Francisco, City Lights Books, 1986. **18.** BATAILLE, GEORGES, **Visions of Excess**, Selected Writings, Stoekl, Allan, trans., Minneaopolis, Universtiy of Minnesota Press, 1985. **19.** BATCHEN, GEOFFREY, BURNING WITH DESIRE. **The Conception of Photography**, Cambridge MA, MIT Press, 1997. **20.** BATESON, GREGORY, **Steps to an Ecology of Mind**, Chicago, The University of Chicago Press, 1972. **21.** BENJAMIN, WALTER, **Illuminations**, London, Pimlico, 1999. **22.** BENJAMIN, WALTER, **One Way Street**, London, Verso, 1997. **23.** BERGER, JOHN, **Ways of Seeing**, New York, Penguin Books, 1972. **24.** BERGSON, HENRI, **Creative Evolution**, New York, Dover Publications, 1998. **25.** BERGSON, HENRI, **Matter and Memory**, New York, Zone Books, 1988. **26.** BERGSON, HENRI, **The Creative Mind: An Introduction to Metaphysics**, New York, Citadel Press, 2002. **27.** BEVAN, ROBERT, **The Destruction of Memory – Architecture at War**, UK, Reaktion Books, 2006. **28.** BHABHA, HOMI K., **The Location of Culture**, London, Routledge, 1994. **29.** BIDNER, STEFAN, THOMAS FEUERSTEIN, EDS., **Sample Minds: Materials on Sampling Culture**, Koeln, Verlag der Buchhandlung Walther Koenig, 2005. **30.** BILLINGHAM, PETER, **Sensing the City through Television. Urban identities in fictional drama**, Bristol, UK and Portland OR, Intellect Books, 2003. **31.** BLOM, INA, **On the Style Site, Art, Sociality, and Media Culture**, New York, Sternberg Press, 2007. **32.** BONIFACE, SIMON, ZIEMANN, ULF, EDS., **Plasticity in the Human Nervous System: Investigations with Transcranial Magnetic Stimulation**, New York, Cambridge University Press, 2003. **33.** BORDWELL, DAVID AND COWARD, NOEL, **Post-Theory: Reconstructing Film Studies**, USA, University of Wisconsin Press, 1996. **34.** BORRIES, FRIEDRICH VON, WALZ, P., AND BÖTTGER, STEFFEN, EDS., **Space Time Play**, Switzerland, Birkhäuser Verlag AG, 2007. **35.** BOSQUET, ALAIN, **Conversations With Salvador Dali**, New York, E.P. Dutton and Co., 1969. **36.** BOVIER, LINOEL AND PERRET, MAI-THU, **Timewave Zero**, Jap Editions/ Revolver/Grazer Kunstverein, 2001. **37.** BRACKENRIDGE, CRAIG, **Hell's bent on Rockin'. A History of Psychobilly**, London, Cherry Red Books, 2007. **38.** BRAUDY, LEO AND COHEN, MARSHALL, **Film Theory and Criticism**, Oxford, Oxford University Press, 1999. **39.** BROWN, TRISHA, **So that the Audience does not know whether I have stopped Dancing**, Minneapolis, Minnesota, Exhibition Catalogue, Walker Art Center, 2008. **40.** BRUNO, GIULIANA, **Atlas of Emotion. Journeys in Art, Architecture and Film**, New York, Verso, 2002. **41.** BRUNO, GIULIANA, **Public Intimacy. Architecture and the Visual Art**, Cambridge MA, MIT Press, 2007. **42.** BRYSON, NORMAN, **Vision and Painting: The Logic of the Gaze**, New Haven CT, London UK, Yale University Press, 1983. **43.** BUCHANAN, IAN AND LAMBERT, GREGG, **Deleuze and Space. Deleuze Connections**, University of Toronto Press, North America, Edingburgh Press 2005. **44.** BULL, MICHAEL AND BACK, LES, EDS., **The Auditory Culture Reader**, New York, Berg Publishers, 2003. **45.** BULLER, DAVID. J, ADAPTING MINDS, **Evolutionary Psychology and the Persistent Quest**, Cambridge MA, MIT Press, 2005. **46.** BURGER, PETER, **Theory of the Avante Garde, Minneapolis**, University of Minnesota Press, 1984. **47.** CACIOPPO, JOHN T. AND BERNSTON, GARY G., EDS., **Essays in Social Neuroscience**, Cambridge MA, MIT Press, 2004. **48.** CACIOPPO, JOHN T., VISSER, PENNY S., AND PICKETT, CYNTHIA L., EDS., **Social Neuroscience, People thinking about**

thinking people, Cambridge MA, MIT Press, 2006. **49.** CALDWELL, W. V., **LSD Psychotherapy An Exploration of Psychedelic and Psycholytic Therapy** , New York, Grove Press, 1968. **50.** CASTELLS, MANUEL, **The Rise of the Network Society**, UK, Blackwell Publishing, 1996. **51.** CHANGEAUX, JEAN PIERRE, **Neuronal Man: The Biology of Mind**, Princeton, Princeton University Press, 1985. **52.** CHANGEAUX, JEAN PIERRE, **The Physiology of Truth: Neuroscience and Human Knowledge**, London, The Belknap Press of Harvard University Press, 2004. **53.** CHANGEUX, JEAN-PIERRE AND CHAVAILLON, JEAN, EDS., **Origins of the Human Brain**, Foundation Fyssen, UK, Clarendon Press, 1996. **54.** CHEROUX, CLEMENT, APRAXINE, PIERRE, FISCHER, ANDREAS, CANGUILHEM, DENIS, AND SCHMIT, SOPHIE, **The Perfect Medium: Photography and the Occult**, Exhibition Catalogue, New York, The Metropolitan Museum of Art New York, 2005. **55.** CHURCHLAND, PATRICIA, **Neurophilosophy: Toward a Unified Science of the Mind-Brain**, Cambridge MA, MIT Press, 1989. **56.** CLARKE, ARTHUR C., **2001: A Space Odyssey**, London, BCA, 1997. **57.** CLARKE, EDWIN AND JACYNA, L.S., **Nineteenth Century Origins of Neuroscientific Concepts**, Berkeley, University of California Press, 1987. **58.** CLEEREMANS, AXEL, ED., **The Unity of Consciousness: Binding, Integration and Dissociation**, New York, Oxford University Press, 2003. **59.** CLOKE, PAUL AND JOHNSTON, RON, EDS., **Spaces of Geographical Thought: Deconstructing Human Geography's Binaries**, London, Sage Publications, 2005. **60.** COLES, ALEX, **The Optic of Walter Benjamin**, UK, Black Dog Publishing, 1999. **61.** COLOMINA, BEATRIZ, **Privacy and Publicity**, Cambridge MA, MIT press, 1996. **62.** CONNOLLY, WILLIAM E., **Neuropolitics: Thinking, Culture, Speed**, Minneapolis, University of Minnesota Press, 2002. **63.** CRARY, JONATHAN, **Suspensions of Perception: Attention, Spectacle, and Modern Culture**, Cambridge and London, MIT Press, 1999. **64.** CRARY, JONATHAN, **Techniques of the Observer**, Cambridge MA, MIT Press, 1990. **65.** DEACON, TERRENCE W., **The Symbolic Species: The Co-evolution of Language and the Brain**, New York, W. W. Norton and Company, 1997. **66.** DEBAENE, STANISLAS, **The Number Sense – How the mind creates Mathematics**, USA, Oxford University Press, 1997. **67.** DE BOLLA, PETER, **The Education of the Eye: Painting, Landscape, and Architecture in Eighteenth-Century Britain**, Stanford, Stanford University Press, 2003. **68.** DEBORD, GUY, **Complete Cinematic Works**. Scripts, Stills, Documents, Knabb, Ken, trans., ed., California US, Ak Press, 2004. **69.** DEBORD, GUY, **Society of the Spectacle**, Detroit, Black and Red, 1983. **70.** DECOSTERD, JEAN-GILLES AND RAHM, PHILIPPE, **Physiological Architecture**, Basel, Birkhauser, 2002. **71.** DEHAENE, STANISLAS, ED., **The Cognitive Neuroscience of Consciousness**, London, MIT Press, 2001. **72.** DEHAENE, STANISLAS, DUHAMEL, JEAN-RENE, HAUSER, MARC. D, AND RIZZOLATTI, GIACOMO, EDS., **From Monkey Brain to Human Brain**, Cambridge MA and London UK, A Bradford Book, The MIT Press, 2005. **73.** DELANDA, MANUEL, **A Thousand Years of Nonlinear History**, New York, Swerve Editions, 1997. **74.** DELANDA, MANUEL, **Intensive Science and Virtual Philosophy**, London, Continuum, 2002. **75.** DELEUZE, GILLES, **Cinema 1: The Movement Image**, Minneapolis, University of Minnesota Press, 1995. **76.** DELEUZE, GILLES, **Cinema 2: The Time Image**, Minneapolis, University of Minnesota Press, 1995. **77.** DELEUZE, GILLES, **Difference & Repetition**, Patton, Paul, trans., New York, Columbia University Press, 1994. **78.** DELEUZE, GILLES, **Foucault**, Minneapolis, University of Minnesota Press, 1988. **79.** DELEUZE, GILLES, **The Fold: Leibniz and the Baroque**, Minneapolis, The University of Minnesota Press, 1993. **80.** DELEUZE, GILLES AND GUATTARI, FELIX, **Anti-Oedipus: Capitalism and Schizophrenia**, Minneapolis, University of Minnesota Press, 1994. **81.** DELEUZE, GILLES AND GUATTARI, FELIX, **On the Line**, New York, Semiotext, 1983. **82.** DELEUZE, GILLES AND GUATTARI, FELIX, **What is Philosophy**, London,Verso, 1994. **83.** DE QUINCEY, THOMAS, **Confessions of an English Opium-Eater**, Oxford, Oxford University Press, reissued as Oxford World's Classic, 1998. **84.** DIDI-HUBERMAN, GEORGES, **Invention of Hysteria: Charcot and the Photographic Iconography of the Salpetriere**, London, MIT Press, 2003. **85.** DODGE, MARTIN AND ROB KITCHIN, **Mapping Cyberspace**, London and New York Routledge, 2001. **86.** DUPOUX, EMMANUEL, **Language, Brain, and Cognitive Development**, Cambridge MA, MIT Press, 2001. **87.** EASTERLING, KELLER, **Enduring Innocence. Global architecture and its political masquerades**, Cambridge MA, MIT Press, Massachusetts, USA, 2005. **88.** EDELMAN, GERALD M., **Consciousness. How Matter Becomes Imagination**, UK, Penguin Books 2001. **89.** EDELMAN, GERALD, **Neural Darwinism**, New York, Basic Books, 1987. **90.** EDELMAN, GERALD, **Remembered Present**, New York, Basic Books, 1994. **91.** EDELMAN, GERALD M. AND TONONI, GIULIO, **A Universe of Consciousness: How Matter becomes Imagination**, New York, Basic Books, 2000. **92.** EDWARDS, ELISABETH, GOSDEN, CHRIS, AND PHILLIPS, RUTH B., EDS., **Sensible Objects, Colonialism, Museums and Material Culture**, New York and Oxford, Berg Publishers, 2006. **93.** EISENMAN, PETER, **Barefoot on White-Hot Walls**, Noever, Peter, eds., Germany, Hatje Cantz Verlag, 2005. **94.** EISENMAN, PETER, **Blurred Zones, Investigation of the Interstitial**, New York, Monacelli Press, 2003. **95.** EISENMAN, PETER, **Inside Out, Selected Writings 1963-1988**, New Haven and London, Yale Universtiy Press, 2004. **96.** EISENSTEIN, SERGEI, **The Film Sense**, London, Boston, Faber and Faber, 1986. **97.** ESPOSITO,

ROBERTO, **Biopolitics and Philosophy**, Campbell, Timothy, trans., Minneapolis, London, University of Minnesota Press, 2008. **98.** **Exhibiton Catalogue, Design and the Elastic Mind**, New York, The Museum of Modern Art, 2008. **99.** **Exhibition Catalogue, New York Collection for Stockholm**, Stockholm, Moderna Museet, 1973. **100.** FERNANDEZ-GALIANO, **Fire and Memory. On Architecture and Energy**, Carino, Gina, trans., Cambridge MA, MIT Press 2000. **101.** FLAXMAN, GREGORY, ED., **The Brain is the Screen: Deleuze and the Philosophy of Cinema**, Minneapolis, University of Minnesota Press, 2000. **102.** FLUSSER, VILEM, **The Shape of Things. A Philosophy of Design**, UK, Reaktion Books, 1999. **103.** FOLLIN, FRANCES, **Embodied Visions: Bridget Riley, Op Art and the Sixties**, New York, Thames and Hudson, 2004. **104.** FOSTER, HAL, ED., **Vision and Visuality**, Dia Art Foundation, New York, Bay Press, 1985. **105.** FOUCAULT, MICHEL, **The Archaeology of Knowledge**, London, Routledge, 2005. **106.** FRAMPTON, DANIEL, **Filmosophy**, London & New York, Wallflower Press, 2006. **107.** FRAMPTON, KENNETH, **Le Corbusier**, London & New York, Thames and Hudson, 2001. **108.** FREUD, SIGMUND, **Civilization and its Discontents**, Riviere, Joan, trans., New York, Dover Publications, 1994. **109.** FREUD SIGMUND, **The Interpretation of Dreams**, The Standard Edition, Strachey, James, trans., New York, Avon Books, 1965. **110.** FREUD, SIGMUND, **Totem and Taboo**, London, Routledge, 1950. **111.** FRITH, CHRISTOPHER AND WOLPERT, DANIEL, EDS., **The Neuroscience of Social Interaction. Decoding, Imitating, and Influencing the Actions of Others**, Oxford University Press, USA 2004, The Royal Society 2003. **112.** FUSTER, JOAQUIN M., **Cortex and Mind: Unifying Cognition**, New York, Oxford University Press, 2003. **113.** FUSTER, JOACHIM M., **Memory in the Cerebral Cortex**, Cambridge MA, MIT Press, 1995. **114.** GAGE, JOHN, **Colour and Culture. Practice and Meaning from Antiquity to Abstraction**, London, Thames and Hudson, 1995. **115.** GAZZANIGA, MICHAEL, The Cognitive Neurosciences, Cambridge MA, MIT Press, 1995. **116.** GIBSON, JAMES J., **The Ecological Approach to Visual Perception**, Hillsdale New Jersey, Lawrence Erlbaum Associates, 1986. **117.** GIEDION, SIGFRIED, **Space, Time and Architecture, the growth of a new tradition**, Cambridge MA, Harvard University Press, 1967. **118.** GLIMCHER, PAUL W., **Decisions, Uncertainty, and the Brain. The Science of Neuroeconomics**, Cambridge Massachusetts, London UK, A Bradford Book, The MIT Press, 2004. **119.** GOETHE, WOLFGANG JOHANN VON, **Theory of Colours**, Cambridge MA, MIT Press, 1970. **120.** GOMBRICH, E.H., **Art and Illusion**, Princeton NJ, Princeton University Press, 1961. **121.** GRAHAM, DAN, **Two-Way Mirror Power: Selected Writings by Dan Graham on his Art**, Cambridge MA, MIT Press, 1999. **122.** GREGORY, R.L., **Eye and Brain: The Psychology of Seeing**, London, World University Library, 1966. **123.** GROSZ, ELIZABETH, **Architecture From the Outside**, Cambridge Massachusetts, MIT Press, 2001. **124.** GROSZ, ELIZABETH, **Space, Time, Perversion**, London, Routledge, 1995. **125.** GROYS, BORIS, **Art Power**, Cambridge Massachusetts, The MIT Press, Cambridge Massachusetts, 2008. **126.** GRUNENBERG, CHRISTOPH, **Summer of Love – Psychedelische Kunst der 60er Jahre**, Germany, Hatje Cantz, 2005. **127.** GUATTARI, FELIX, **Chaosophy**, New York, Semiotext, 1995. **128.** GUATTARI, FELIX AND ROLNIK, SUELY, **Molecular Revolution in Brazil**, Los Angeles, Semiotext(e), 2008. **129.** HAMMERSTEIN, PETER, **Genetic and Cultural Evolution of Cooperation**, Cambridge MA, MIT Press, 2005. **130.** HARPIGNIES, J.P., ED., CONTRIBUTIONS BY TERENCE MC KENNA, ANDREW WEIL, ALEX GREY, KAT HARRISON, AND OTHERS, **Visionary Plant Consciousness, the Shamanic Teachings of the Plant World**, Rochester, Vermont, Park Street Press, 2007. **131.** HAYLES, KATHERINE N., **How we became Posthuman, Virtual Bodies in Cybernetics, Literature, and Informatics**, Chicago and London, The University of Chicago Press, 1999. **132.** HEBB, D.O., **The Organization of Behavior. A Neuropsychologic Theory**, Wiley UK, 1949. **133.** HEBDIGE, DICK, **Cut 'N' Mix**, London, Routledge, 1987. **134.** HEGEL, G.W.F., **Phenomenology of Sprit**, Miller, A.V., trans., London, Oxford University Press, 1977. **135.** HEIDEGGER, MARTIN, **Poetry, Language, Thought**, New York, Harper and Row, 1975. **136.** HEIDEGGER, MARTIN, **The Question Concerning Technology and Other Essays**, New York, Harper Colophon Books, 1977. **137.** HENDRIX, JOHN SHANNON, **Architecture and Psychoanalysis, Peter Eisenman and Jacques Lacan**, New York, Peter Lang Publishing, 2006. **138.** HEYNEN, HILDE, **Architecture and Modernity**, Cambridge MA, MIT Press, 1999. **139.** HOFMAN, M.A., BOER, G.J., HOLTMAAT, A.J.G.D., VAN SOMEREN, E.J.W., VERHAAGEN, J., AND SWAAB, D. F., EDS., **Plasticity in the Adult Brain: From Genes to Neurotherapy, Progress in Brain Research**, Volume 138., Amsterdam, London, New York, Elsevier Science, 2002. **140.** HOWES, DAVID, **Empire of the Senses. The Sensual Culture Reader**, New York, Berg Publishers, 2005. **141.** HUNDERT, EDWARD M., **Philosophy, Psychiatry and Neuroscience, Three Approaches to the Mind, A Synthetic Ananlysis of the Varieties of Human Experience**, US, UK, Clarendon Paperbacks, 1990. **142.** HUTTENLOCHER, PETER R., **Neural Plasticity: The Effects of Environment on the Development of the Cerebral Cortex**, London, Harvard University Press, 2002. **143.** INGOLD, TIM, **The Perception of the Environment, Essays in Livelihood, Dwelling and Skill**, London, Routledge, 2000. **144.** JACOBS, STEVEN, **The Wrong House: The Architecture of Alfred Hitchcock**, Rotterdam, 010 Publishers, 2007. **145.** JAMESON, FREDRIC, **Postmodernism, or, The**

Cultural Logic of Late Capitalism, Durham NC, Duke University Press, 1991. **146.** JAY, MARTIN, **Downcast Eyes**, Berkeley, University of California Press, 1993. **147.** JOHNSON, MARK H., ED., **Brain Development and Cognition: A Reader**, Oxford, Blackwell Publishers, 1993. **148.** JONES, AMELIA, **Irrational Modernism, A Neurasthenic History of New York Dada**, Cambridge MA, MIT Press, 2004. **149.** KAAS, JON H., **The Mutable Brain: Dynamic and Plastic Features of the Developing and Mature Brain**, Amsterdam, Hardwood Academic publishers, 2001. **150.** KAPROW, ALLAN, **Essays on the Blurring of Art and Life**, Kelly, Jeff, ed., Berkeley, University of California Press, 2003. **151.** KELSO, J. A. SCOTT, **Dynamic Patterns: The Self Organization of Brain and Behavior**, Cambridge MA, MIT Press, 1997. **152.** KEPES, GYORGY, **Language of Vision**, Chicago, Theobold, 1944. **153.** KEYES, CHERYL. L., **Rap Music and Street Consciousness, Urbana and Chicago**, University of Illinois Press, 2004. **154.** KILLEN, ANDREAS, **Berlin Electropolis; Shock, Nerves and German Modernity**, USA and London UK, University of California Press, 2006. **155.** KITCHIN, ROB AND BLADES, MARK, **The Cognition of Geographic Space**, London and New York, I.B. Taurus, 2002. **156.** KITTLER, FRIEDRICH A., **Gramophone, Film, Typewriter**, Stanford, Stanford University Press, 1999. **157.** KLEIN, NORMAN M., **The Vatican to Vegas: a History of Special Effects**, New York, New Press, 2004. **158.** KLINGMANN ANNA, **Brandscapes – Architecture in the Experience Economy**, Cambridge, Massachusetts, London UK, The MIT Press, 2007. **159.** KOCH, CHRISTOF, **The quest for Consciousness – A Neurobiological Approach**, Colorado, Roberts & Company Publishers, 2004. **160.** KOLB, BRYAN, **Brain Plasticity and Behavior**, New Jersey, Lawrence Erlbaum Associates Publishers, 1995. **161.** KOOLHAAS, REM, **Mutations: Harvard project on the City**, Bordeaux, Actar, 2001. **162.** KOOLHAAS, REM, BOERI, STEPHANO, KWINTER, SANFORD, TAZI, NADJA, AND OBRIST, HANS ULRICH, **Mutations**, Actar Publishers, Arc Enreve Centre d'Architecture. **163.** KRAUSS, ROSALIND, **The Optical Unconscious**, Cambridge MA, October Books, MIT Books, 1995. **164.** KRAUSS, ROSALIND, **The Originality of the Avant-Garde and Other Modernist Myths**, Cambridge MA, MIT Press, 1986. **165.** KUBLER, GEORGE, **The Shape of Time, Remarks on the History of Things**, New Haven, CT, Yale University Press, 1962. **166.** KUBO, MICHAEL AND ALBERT FERRE, **Phylogenesis: FOA's Ark, Foreign Office Architects**, Barcelona, Actar, 2003. **167.** KUDIELKA, ROBERT, ED., **The Eye's Mind: Bridget Riley, Collected Writings 1965-1999**. London, Thames and Hudson, 1999. **168.** LACAN, JACQUES, **Ecrits: A Selection**, London, Routledge, 1989. **169.** LACAN, JACQUES, **The Four Fundamental Concepts of Psychoanalysis**, trans. Sheridan, Alan, New York, W.W. Norton, 1981. **170.** LACAN, JACQUES, **The Language of the Self: The Function of Language in Psychoanalysis**, Wilden, Anthony, trans., Baltimore and London, Johns Hopkins University Press, 1968. **171.** LASZLO, ERVIN, **The Systems View of the World**, New York, George Braziller, Eighth Printing, 1988. **172.** LATOUR, BRUNO, **Reassembling the Social. An Introduction to Actor-Network-Theory**, New York, Oxford University Press, 2005. **173.** LATOUR, BRUNO, **We Have Never been Modern**, Cambridge MA, Harvard University Press, 2008. **174.** LEE, PAMELA M., **Chronophobia: On time in the Art of the 1960's**, London, MIT Press, 2004. **175.** LEFEBVRE, HENRI, **Rhythmanalysis: Space, Time and Everyday Life**, Continuum Press, 2004. **176.** LEFEBVRE, HENRI AND NICHOLSON-SMITH, DONALD, **The Production of Space**, UK, Blackwells, 1991. **177.** LEIBNIZ, G. W., **Discourse on Metaphysics and The Monadology**, Mineola, New York, Dover Publications. **178.** LEROI-GOURHAN, ANDRE, **Gesture and Speech**, Bostock Berger, Anna, trans., The MIT Press, Cambridge, Massachusetts, London, UK, 1993. **179.** LEVINSON, STEPHEN C. AND JAISSON, PIERRE, EDS., **Evolution and Culture**, Cambridge, Massachusetts, MIT Press, 2006. **180.** LEVY, DANIEL AND SZNAIDER NATAN, **The Holocost and Memory in the Global Age**, by Oksiloff, Assenka, trans., Frankfurt, Suhrkamp Verlag 2006. **181.** LEVY, PIERRE, **Becoming Virtual: Reality in the Digital Age**, New York, Plenum Press, 1998. **182.** LEWIS-WILLIAMS, DAVID, **The Mind in the Cave**, London, Thames and Hudson, 2002. **183.** LIBET, BENJAMIN, **Mind Time. The Temporal Factor in Consciousness**, Harvard University Press, 2004. **184.** LIEBERMAN, PHILIP, **Human Language and Our Reptilian Brain**, Harvard University Press, 2000. **185.** LIND, MARIA AND MINICHBAUER, RAIMUND, EDS., **European Cultural Policies 2015**, Iaspis, Stockholm, International Art Studio, 2005. **186.** LLINAS, RODOLFO R., **I of the Vortex: From Neurons to Self**, Cambridge, Massachusetts, MIT Press, 2001. **187.** LLINAS, RODOLFO AND CHURCHLAND, PATRICIA, **The Mind-Brain Continuum**, Massachusetts USA, MIT Press, 1996. **188.** LUHMANN, NIKLAS, **Art as a Social System**, Knodt, Eva M., trans., Stanford, Stanford University Press, 2000. **189.** LUHMANN, NIKLAS, **Social Systems**, Bednarz, John, trans., Stanford, Stanford University Press, 1984. **190.** LYNCH, KEVIN, **The Image of the City**, Cambridge Massachusetts, The MIT Press, 1960. **191.** LYNN, GREG, **Animate Form**, New York, Princeton Architectural Press, 1999. **192.** LYOTARD, JEAN-FRANCOIS, **The Inhuman**, Stanford, Stanford University Press, 1988. **193.** LYOTARD, JEAN-FRANCOIS, **The Postmodern Condition: A Report on Knowledge**, Manchester, Manchester University Press, 2004. **194.** MCDONOUGH, TOM, ED., **Guy Debord and the Situationist International; Texts and Documents**, Massachusetts USA, An October Book, The MIT

Press, 2004. **195.** MACKENZIE, ADRIAN, **Transductions: Bodies and Machines at Speed**, London, Continuum Press, 2002. **196.** MC KENZIE, WARK, **A Hacker Manifesto**, Cambridge Massachusetts, London, Harvard University Press, 2004. **197.** MACPHEE, GRAHAM, **The Architecture of the Visible**, London, New York, Continuum, 2002. **198.** MAILLET, ARNAUD, **The Claude Glass; Use and Meaning of the Black Mirror in Western Art**, New York, Zone Books, 2004. **199.** MARIJUAN, PEDRO C. ED., **Cajal and Consciousness: Scientific Approaches to Conciousness on the Centennial of Ramon y Cajal's Birth**, New York, New York Academy of Sciences, volume 929, 2001. **200.** MARTIN, REINHOLD, **The Organizational Complex. Architecture, Media, and Corporate Space**, Massachusetts, USA, MIT Press, 2003. **201.** MASSUMI, BRIAN, **Parables for the Virtual: Movement, Affect, Sensation**, Durham USA, London UK, Duke University Press, 2002. **202.** MATSUDA, MATT K., **The Memory of the Modern**, Oxford University Press, New York, 1996. **203.** MATURANA, HUMBERTO R. AND VARELA, FRANCISCO, **The Tree of Knowledge: The Biological roots of Human Understanding**, Boston and London, Shambala Publications, 1987. **204.** MBEMBE, ACHILLE, **On the Postcolony**, Berkeley, University of California Press, 2001. **205.** MEARLEAU-PONTY, MAURICE, **Phenomenology of Perception**, Routledge, 1962. **206.** MERLEAU-PONTY, MAURICE, **Sense and Non-Sense**, Northwestern University Studies in Phenomonenonlogy and Existential Philosophy, Dreyfus, Hubert L. & Patricia Allen, USA, Northwestern University Press, 1964. **207.** MEARLEAU-PONTY, MAURICE, **The Primacy of Perception**, USA, Northwestern University Press, 1964. **208.** MIESSEN, MARKUS AND BASAR, SHUMON, EDS., **Did Someone say Participate? An Atlas of Spatial Practice**, Massachusetts, The MIT Press, 2006. **209.** MILLER, JACQUES-ALAIN, ED., **The four Fundamental Concepts of Psychoanalysis. The Seminar of Jancques Lacan Book XI.**, Sheridan, Alan, trans., New York, W. W, Norton & Company, 1998. **210.** MINSKY, MARVIN, **The Society of Mind**, New York, Simon and Schuster, 1988. **211.** MIRZOEFF, NOCHOLAS, ED., **The Visual Culture Reader**, London, Routledge, 1998. **212.** MITCHELL, W.J. T., **What do Pictures Mean**, University of Chicago Press, 2005. **213.** MITHEN, STEPHEN, **The Prehistory of the Mind; The Cognitive Origins of Art and Science**, London, Thames and Hudson, 1996. **214.** NEGRI, ANTONIO, **Marx beyond Marx. Lessons on the Grundrisse**, Autonomedia Inc. USA and Pluto Press UK, 1991. **215.** NEGRI, ANTONIO AND HARDT, MICHAEL, **Empire**, Cambridge, Harvard University Press, 2000. **216.** NOE, ALVA, ED., **Is the World a Grand Illusion**, USA, Imprint Academic, 2002. **217.** NYMAN, MICHAEL, **Experimental Music; Cage and Beyond**, New York, Schirmer Books, 1981. **218.**

O'DOHERTY, BRIAN, **Inside the White Cube. The Ideology of the Gallery Space**, Expanded Edition, California, London UK, University of California Press, 1986. **219.** PAKALUK, MICHAEL, **Aristotle's Nicomachean Ethics, an Introduction, Cambridge Introductions to Key Philosophical Texts**, Cambridge, Cambridge University Press, 2005. **220.** PASHLER, HAROLD E., **The Psychology of Attention**, Cambridge, MIT Press, 1998. **221.** PEREC, GEORGE, **Species of Spaces and Other Pieces, revised edition**, London, Penguin Books, 1999. **222.** PEREZ-GOMEZ, ALBERTO, **Architecture and the Crisis of Modern Science**, Massachusetts, MIT press, 1983. **223.** PERNIOLA, MARIO, **Art and its shadow**, Verdiccio, Massimo, ed., New York, London, Continuum, 2004. **224.** PLANT, SADIE, **Writing on Drugs**, London, Faber and Faber limited, 1999. **225.** POGGIOLI, RENATO, **The Theory of the Avant-Garde**, Belknap Press, 2003. **226.** POPPER, FRANK, **Origins and Development of Kinetic Art**, Bann, Stephen, trans., England, Studio Vista, 1968. **227.** RAJCHMAN, JOHN, **The Deleuze Connections**, Cambridge: MIT Press, 2000. **228.** RANCIERE, JACQUES, **The Flesh of Words**. The Politics of Writing, Mandell, Charlotte, trans., California, USA, Stanford University Press, 2004. **229.** RANCIERE, JACQUES, **The Future of the Image**, Elliot, Gregory, trans. London, New York, Verso, 2007. **230.** REISER + UMEMOTO, **Atlas of Novel Tectonics**, New York, Princeton Architectural Press, 2006. **231.** REYNA, STEPHEN P., **Connections: Brain, Mind, and Culture in Social Anthropology**, London, Routledge 2002. **232.** RICHERSON, PETER J., BOYD, ROBERT, **Not By Genes Alone**, University of Chicago Press, 2005. **233.** RIEBER, ROBERT W. AND ROBINSON, DAVID K., **The Essential Vygotsky**, New York, Kluwer Academic/Plenum Publishers, 2004. **234.** ROSS, KRISTIN, **The Emergence of Social Space. Rimbaud and the Paris Commune**, London, New York, Verso 2008. **235.** ROWE, COLIN, **Collage City**, Cambridge, Massachusetts, MIT Press, 1984. **236.** ROWE, COLIN, **The Mathematics of the Ideal Villa and Other Essays**, Cambridge, Massachusetts, The MIT Press, 1987. **237.** SADLER, SIMON, **The Situationist City**, The MIT Press, Cambridge, Massachusetts, London UK, 1999. **238.** SAUSSURE, FERDINAND, **Course in General Linguistics**, Baskin, Wade, trans., New York, McGraw Hill, 1966. **239.** SCHIMMEL, PAUL AND MARK, LISA, **Ecstasy: In and about altered States**, The MIT Press, 2005. **240.** SCHWARZER, MITCHELL, **Zoom Scape. Architecture in Motion and Media**, New York, Princeton Architectural Press, 2004. **241.** SCOTT, FELICITY D., **Architecture or Techno-utopia. Politics after Modernism**, Massachusetts, MIT Press, 2007. **242.** SIMMEL, GEORG, **On Indiviuality and Social Forms**, Levine, Donald N. intro, ed., Chicago and London, The University of Chicago Press, 1971. **243.** SIMONDON, GILBERT,

Du Mode d'existence des Objets Techniques, France, Aubier, 2001. **244.** SOLMS, MARK AND TURNBULL, OLIVER, **The Brain and The Inner World: An Introduction to the Neuroscience of Subjective Experience**, New York, Other Press, 2002. **245.** SPORNS, OLAF, TONONI, GIULIO, EDS., **Selectionism and the Brain, London**, Academic Press, 1994. **246.** SPUYBROEK, LARS, **Nox**, London, Thames and Hudson, 2004. **247.** STAFFORD, BARBARA MARIA, **Visual Analogy: Consciousness as the Art of Connecting**, Cambridge, MIT Press, 1999. **248.** STALLABRASS, JULIAN, **Art Incorporated; the Story of Contemporary Art**, USA, Oxford University Press, 2004. **249.** STAMENOV, MAXIM I. AND GALLESE,VITTORIO, EDS., **Mirror Neurons and the Evolution of Brain and Language, Advances in Consciousness Research**, John Benjamins Publishing Company, 2002. **250.** STIEGLER, BERNARD, **Technics and Time: The Fault of Epimetheus**, Stanford, Stanford University Press, 1998. **251.** TEMPKIN, ANN, **Color Chart: Reinventing Color, 1959 to Today, Exhibition Catalogue**, New York, The Museum of Modern Art, 2008. **252.** TERRANOVA, TIZIANA, **Network Culture. Politics for the Informational Age**, Pluto Press London, 2004. **253. Texte zur Kunst: Artists' Artists**, Magazine, No 71, September Issue, Berlin, 2008. **254.** THOMAS, MICAL, ED., **Surrealism and Architecture**, Routledge, London, 2005. **255.** TSCHUMI, BERNARD, **Architecture and Disjunction**, Cambridge USA, The MIT Press, London England, 1996. **256.** VAN OOYEN, ARJEN, ED., **Modeling Neural Development**, London and Massachusetts, MIT Press, 2003. **257.** VARELA, FRANCISCO J., THOMPSON, EVAN, ROSCH, ELEANOR, **The Embodied Mind**, Massachusetts, MIT Press, 1993. **258.** VIDLER, ANTHONY, **Warped Space:Art, Architecture and Anxiety in Modern Culture**, Massachusetts, MIT Press, 2000. **259.** VIRILIO, PAUL, **Lost Dimension**, USA, Semiotext(e), 1991. **260.** VIRILIO, PAUL, **The Vision Machine**, London: British Film Institute, Indiana:Indiana University Press, 1994. **261.** VIRNO, PAOLO, **Multitude; between Innovation and Negation**, Bertoletti, Isabella, Cascaito, James, and Casson, Andrea, trans., Semiotext(e) 2008. **262.** VIRNO, PAOLO AND BERTOLETTI, ISABELLA, **The Grammar of the Multitude**, USA, Semiotext, Foreign Agent Series, 2004. **263.** VYGOTSKY, L.S., **Mind in Society. The Development of Higher Psychological Processes**, Cole, Michal, John-Steiner, Vera, Scribner, Sylvia, and Souberman, Ellen, eds., Cambridge Massachusetts, London UK, Havard University Press, 1978. **264.** WALLENSTEIN, SVEN-OLOV, **Essays, Lectures**, Stockholm, Axl Books, 2007. **265.** WEBER, BRUCE H. AND DEPEW, DAVID J., EDS., **Evolution and Learning: The Baldwin Effect Reconsidered**, Cambridge, MIT Press, 2003. **266.** WEISS, ALLEN S., **Phantasmic Radio**, USA, Duke University Press, 1995. **267.** WEIZMAN, EYAL,

Hollow Land, Israel's Architecture of Occupation, London,Verso, 2007. **268.** WERTSCH, JAMES V., **Vygotsky and the Social Formation of Mind**, Cambridge Massachusetts, London UK, Harvard University Press, 1988. **269.** WERTSCH, JAMES V., DEL RIO, PABLO, AND ALVAREZ, AMELIA, **Sociocultural Studies of Mind**, USA, UK, Cambridge University Press, 1995. **270.** WEXLER, BRUCE E., **Brain and Culture. Neurobiology, Ideology and Social Change**, Cambridge Massachusetts, London UK, The MIT Press, A Bradford Book, 2006. **271.** WILLIAMS, RAYMOND, **Television**, London, Routledge, 1990. **272.** ZIZEK, SLAVOJ, **Organs Without Bodies, On Deleuze and Consequences**, New York, London, Routledge, 1994. **273.** ZIZEK, SLAVOJ, **Welcome to the Desert of the Real**, London, Verso, 2002. **274.** ZWEIFEL, STEFAN, STEINER, JURI, AND STAHLHUT, HEINZ; EDS., **Exhibition Catalogue: In Girum Imus Nocte et consumimur Igni .The Situationist International (1957-1972)**, Museum Tinguely, Basel 2007, Centraal Museum Utrecht, 2006.

Neuro Aesthetic Library,
Berlin

Biography

Warren Neidich is an artist, writer and organizer who currently lives and works in Berlin. His work has been exhibited internationally in such institutions as the Whitney Museum of Art, Palais de Tokyo, Ludwig Museum, Los Angeles County Museum of Art, Walker Art Museum, The Kitchen and P.S.1, MOMA. Seven catalogues and books of his work and writings have been published, including American History Reinvented, Aperture Foundation, 1989; Unknown Artist, Fricke-Schmid, 1993; Camp O.J., DAP, 1996; and Earthling, Pointed Leaf Press, 2005. A collection of his writing, Blow-up: Photography, Cinema and the Brain, was published by DAP in 2003. He has organized many conferences and curated over thirty exhibitions including Conceptual Art as a Neurobiologic Praxis, at the Thread Waxing Space in 1999; Neuroaesthetics, 2005 at Goldsmiths College, London, England; and The Mind in Architecture: From Biopolitics to Noo-politics, at TU Delft, Delft, The Netherlands, 2008. An edited collection of his essays will be published under the same title in 2010 by O10 Press, Rotterdam. He co-produced and founded www.artbrain.org in 1997, as well as founding and editing The Journal of Neuroaesthetics, for which he was an editor until 2008. A selection of residencies and fellowships include: IASPIS Residency, Stockholm, Sweden, 2008; ACE-AHRB Arts and Science Research Fellowship, 2004; Madrid Abierto Public Sculpture Award, 2004; MacDowell Foundation, 1998, Villa Arson, 1994; and Kunstlerhaus Bethanian,1993. He was former Artist in Residence at Goldsmith College and is currently Visiting Scholar at the TU Delft School of Architecture, Delft, Holland.

www.warrenneidich.com

Selected Solo Exhibitions

2009
Galerie Moriarty, Madrid, Spain.

2008
Lost Between the Extensivity / Intensivity Exchange, Onomatopee, Eindhoven, The Netherlands.
Each Rainbow Must Retain the Chromatic Signature, it..., Magnus Müller Gallery, Berlin, Germany.

2006
Earthling 2, Andrew Mummery Gallery, London, England.

2005
Earthling, Michael Steinberg Fine Arts, New York, New York.

2004
Silent: A State of Being, Madrid, Abierto Public Sculpture Competition, Madrid, Spain.

2003
Fröhliche Wissenschaft, Brandenburgischer Kunstverein, Potsdam, Germany.

2002
Warren Neidich: The Mutated Observer, Part 2, California Museum of Photography, Riverside, California.
Warren Neidich: Photographs and Videos, Storefront for Art and Architecture, New York, New York.
Remapping, Edward Mitterand Gallery, Geneva, Switzerland.
Some Stories Concerning the Relations of a Mutated Observer, Gallery Müller De Chiara, Berlin, Germany.

2001
Warren Neidich: The Mutated Observer, Part 1, California Museum of Photography, Riverside, California.
Beyond the Vanishing Point: Los Angeles, Gandy Gallery, Prague, Czech Republic.
The Camp O. J. Installation, Laguna Art Museum, Laguna Beach, California.

2000
Beyond the Vanishing Point: Media and Myth in America, Bayle Art Museum, University of Virginia, Charlottesville, Virginia.

1997
Re-cognition, Steffany Martz Gallery, New York, New York.

1996

Pollock: Holding a Crow With Alchemy, Steffany Martz Gallery, New York, New York.

1994

Cultural Residue, Villa Arson, Nice, France.

1993

Together We Stand / Divided We Fall, Künstlerhaus Bethanien, Berlin, Germany.

1991

Historical Interventions, List Visual Arts Center, M.I.T., Cambridge, Massachusetts.
American History Reinvented, Perspectief Space, Rotterdam, The Netherlands.
The Battle of Chicamauga, Photographic Resource Center, Boston, Massachusetts.

1990

The Kitchen, New York, New York.

1989

American History Reinvented, Aperture Foundation, New York, New York.

Selected Group Exhibitions

2009

The Fax Show, curated by Joao Ribas, The Drawing Center, New York, New York.

2008

Open House, International Artists Studio Program in Sweden (IASPS), Stockholm, Sweden.
Garden of Delights: Yeosu International Art Festival, curated by Raul Zamudio, Yeosu, South Korea.

2007

House Trip, curated by Ami Barak, special exhibition at Artforum Berlin, Germany.
Light and Neon, Edward Mitterand Gallery, Geneva, Switzerland.
Multitasking, curated by Barbara Lauterbach, NGBK, Berlin, continued to:
Stedelijk Museum s'-Hertogenbosch, Netherlands;
Overbeck-Gesellschaft, Lübeck, Germany;
La Filature, Mullhouse, France
Saloon, curated by Adina Popescu, Special Projects Section, Moscow Biennial, Moscow.
My Vision, Reiss-Engelhorn-Museen and Zephyr—Raum für Fotografie, Mannheim, Germany.

2006

Apparatus, curated by Adina Popescu, Program Gallery, Berlin.
The Expanded Eye, curated by Bice Kuriger, Kunsthaus, Zürich, Switzerland.
Protections, curated by Adam Budak and

Christine Peters, Kunsthaus Graz, Graz, Austria.
Sweet Dreams: Contemporary Art and Complicity, curated by Johanna Drucker, Bayle Art Museum, University of Virginia, Charlottesville, Virginia.
Masquerade, curated by Deborah Irmas, Los Angeles California Museum of Art, Los Angeles, California.

2005

Go-Between, curated by Wolfgang Fetz and Peter Lewis, Magazin 4 and Bregenzer Kunstverein, Bregenze, Austria.
Library, Librarie, curated by Idealondon, Institute of Contemporary Art, London, England.
New Labor, curated by Eric Angles, Columbia University Art Gallery, New York, New York.
CAC/tv 12 Hour Performance, curated by Raimundas Malasauskas, Contemporary Arts Center, Vilnius, Lithuania.

2004

Synaesthesia: A Neuro-aesthetic Exhibition, curated by Chloe Vaitsou, Institute of Contemporary Arts, London, England.
Everything is Connected, He, He, He, curated by Gunnar Kvaran, Astrup Fearnley Museum of Modern Art, Oslo, Norway.
Public Execution, curated by Michele Thursz, Anne Ellegood and Defne Ayas, Exit Art, New York, New York.

2003

Harlem Postcards, curated by Christine Kim, Studio Museum of Harlem, New York, New York.

2002

Proper Villians, curated by David Hunt, Artists Space, New Haven, Connecticut.
Charlie Magazine, curated by Bettina Funcke and Maurizio Cattalan, PS1 Contemporary, New York, New York.

2001

Bitstreams, curated by Larry Rinder, Whitney Museum of American Art, New York, New York.
Urban Pornography, curated by Laurie Firstenberg, Artists Space, New York, New York.
Optical Verve, curated by Sylvie Fortin, Ottawa Art Gallery, Ottawa, Canada.
The Reality Effect; Contemporary American Photography, curated by Simon Taylor, Guild Hall, East Hampton, New York.
Video Windows, curated by Lauri Firstenberg, Stux Gallery, New York, New York.

1998

<u>Speed</u>, curated by Bo Modestrand and Hakkan Nilsson, Art Node, Stockholm, Sweden continued to: Bohulans Museum, Uddevalla, Sweden; Galerie Box, Gothenburg, Sweden; Uppsala Konstmuseum, Uppsala, Sweden; Bildmusset, Umea, Sweden.

1997

<u>Notions of the Nineteenth Century</u>, curated by Meg Linton and Tyler Stallings, Huntington Beach Art Center, Huntington, California.
<u>Making It Real</u>, curated by Vik Muniz, Aldrich Museum of Art, Ridgefield, Colorado, continued to: Reykjavik Municipal Art Museum, Reykjavik, Iceland; Bayle Art Museum, Univ. of Virginia, Charlottesville, Virginia; Portland Museum of Art, Portland, Maine; Bakalar Gallery, Massachusetts College of Art, Boston, Massachusetts; Emerson Gallery, Hamilton College, Clinton, New York.

1996

<u>Ports of Entry: William Burroughs</u>, curated by Robert Sobieszek, Los Angeles County Museum of Art, Los Angeles, California and Spencer Museum of Art, Kansas City, Missouri.
<u>Follow the Yellow Brick Road</u>, curated by Martin Kunst, New York Kunsthalle, New York, New York.

1995

<u>Photography After Photography</u>, curated by Hubertus von Amelunxen, Stefan Iglhaut and Florian Rotzer, Aktionsforum Praterinsel, Munich, Germany, continued to: Kunsthalle Krems, Krems, Austria; Stadtische Galerie Erlagen, Erlagen, Germany; Brandenburgische Kunstammlungen, Cottbus, Germany; Musset for Fotokunst, Odense, Denmark; Fotomuseum Winterthur, Winterthur, Switzerland; The Finnish Museum of Photography, Helsinki; Institute of Contemporary Art, Philadelphia, Pennsylvania.

1993

<u>Fontanelle</u>, curated by Christoph Tannert, Potsdam, Germany
<u>Fever</u>, curated by Jeanette Ingberrman and Papo Colo, Exit Art, New York, New <u>Unknown Artist</u>, curated by Michael Wuerthle in collaboration with Martin Kippenberger, Paris Bar, Berlin, Germany.

1992

<u>Salvage Utopia</u>, curated by Paul Bloodgood and Alissa Friedman, AC Project Room, New York, New York.
<u>Relative Truths</u>, curated by Tracey Bashkoff, Guild Hall-East Hampton, New York.
<u>Water Bar</u>, curated by Eric Oppenhiem, Jack Tilton Gallery, New York, New York.
<u>Summer Show</u>, curated by Max Lang, Blum Helman Warehouse, New York, New York.

1991

<u>New York Stories</u>, curated by Richard Wasko, P.S.1 Institute of Contemporary Art, Long Island City, New York.
<u>Des Vessies et des Lanternes</u>, curated by Alain D'hooghe, Palais de Tokyo, Paris, France.

1989

<u>Photography of Invention</u>, curated by Joshua Smith, National Museum of American Art, Washington DC, continued to: The Museum of Contemporary Art, Chicago, Illinois; Walker Museum Of Art, Minneapolis, Minnesota.
<u>Rethinking American Myths</u>, curated by Mathew Postal, Larry Miller Gallery, New York, New York, continued to: University of Connecticut Art Gallery, Stoors, Connecticut; Bard College Art Museum, Annandale-on-Hudson, New York.

1988

<u>Vom Landschaftsbild zur Spurensicherung</u>, curated by Rheinhold Misselbeck, Museum Ludwig, Köln
<u>Television and Art</u>, curated by Mark Miller, Queens Museum, Queens, New York
<u>The Nature of the Real</u>, curated by Renee Ricardo and Paul Laster, White Columns, New York, New York.

Selected Bibliography

2008

Adina Popescu, "Warren Neidich," <u>Artforum International</u>, Summer 2008.
Thea Harold, "In der Werkstatt," <u>Tagesspiegel</u>, Berlin, May 10, 2008.
Christiane Meixner, "Zeigen, was man hat," <u>Tagesspiegel</u>, Berlin, May 3, 2008.
Ana Finel Honigman, "Highway Child at Friedrichshoehe in Berlin," DazedDigital.com, Sept. 4,2008.

2007

Mark Ginsbourne, <u>My Vision – Ideen für die Welt von morgen</u>, exhibition catalogue, 2006.

2006

Maurizio Bortolotti, "Art and Resistance," Domus, December 2006.
Bice Curiger, Expanded Eye, exhibition catalogue, Kunsthaus Graz, 2006.
The Body in Architecture, ed. Deborah Hauptmann, 010 Publishers, 2006.

2005

"Around the Town," The New Yorker, September 19, 2005.
Johanna Drucker, Sweet Dreams: Contemporary Art and Complicity, University of Chicago Press, 2005, 186-197.
Hans Ulrich Obrist, "Warren Neidich," Spot Magazine of the Houston Center of Photography, Spring 2005.
Wolfgang Fetz and Peter Lewis, Go-Between, exhibition catalogue, Magazin 4 and Bregenzer Kunstverein, 2005, 166-174.

2004

Anne Ellegood, "Silent Happenings," Public Execution, exhibition catalogue, Exit Art, 2004.

2003

Miyake Akiko and Hans Ulrich Obrist, Bridge the Gap?, program catalog, Center for Contemporary Art Kitakyusha, 2003.

2002

Sarah Valdez, "Warren Neidich at the Laguna Art Museum," Art in America, February 2002.
Adrian Dannatt, "Brainy," The Art Newspaper, No.128. September 2002, 26-27.
Carlos Brillembourg, "Mirror, Mirror on the Wall," Storefront for Art and Architecture, September 14, 2002.
Sylvie Fortin, Optical Verve, exhibition catalogue, Ottawa Art Gallery, 2002.
Lisa Boone, "Photographs and Distortion," Los Angeles Times, November 7, 2002, weekend section.
Ingebourg Ruthe, "Poelzig und die Kunstvitrine," Berliner Zeitung, February 2002.
Petra Welzel, "Augen auf und durch," Die Tageszeitung, February 26, 2002.

2001

Larry Rinder, "Art in the Digital Age", BitStreams, exhibition catalogue, Whitney Museum of Art, March 2001.
Vivian Letran, "The Natural and the Unnatural," Los Angeles Times, July 27, 2001.
Denise Carvalho, "Bitstreams," Flash Art, May-June 2001.
Christiane Paul, "Hotlist, Artbrain, www.artbrain.org," Artforum, October 2001.

1999

Robert Mahoney, "Millennium at Tate," Time Out, No. 201, July 11–July 17, 2001, 52.
Norman Bryson, "Summer 1999 at Tate", essay for exhibition at Tate Gallery, New York City, July 1999, 4-5.
Regine Basha, "Performing Observations; Recent Work by Warren Neidich," Performance Arts Journal, Spring 1999.
Roberta Smith, "Conceptual Art: Over and Yet Everywhere," The New York Times: Arts and Leisure, April 25, 1999, 1.
"Critics Pick; Alternative, Alternative," Time Out, April 2-9, 1999.

1998

Peter Rostovsky, "Recognition: Steffany Martz Gallery," Zingmagazine, No. 224, December 1998.
"On the Road Again' Jack Kerouac, Photographs by Warren Neidich," The New Yorker, June 22–29, 1998.
Edith Newhall, "Art Feature," New York Magazine, April 28, 1998.
Cathy Lebowitz, "Warren Neidich at Steffany Martz," Art in America, April 1998.

1997

Nancy Princethal, "In the Flow at Franklin Furnace," Art in America, No. 10, October 1997.
Graham Clark, Oxford History of Art: The Photograph, Oxford University Press, Oxford, England, 1997.
Vik Muniz and Luc Sante, Making It Real, exhibition catalogue, Independent Curators International, New York, 1997.

1996

Robert Sobieszek, Ports of Entry: William S. Burroughs and the Arts, exhibition catalogue, Los Angeles Museum of Art, 1996.
Hubertus von Amelunxen, Photography after Photography: Memory and Representation in the Digital Age, Grand Barts, 1996.
"Photography after Photography," Frieze, May 1996, 69.
Robert Mahoney, "Warren Neidich, Pollock Holding a Crow with Alchemy," Time Out, Issue 44, 1996.
Kim Levin, "Art Choices", Village Voice, July 9-16, 1996.
Kim Levin, "Art Short List; Sweat", Village Voice, July 16, 1996, 9.

1994

Susan Kandel, "Slight of Hand," Los Angeles Times, June 9, 1994.

1993

Ulrich Clewing, "Wink mit dem Zaunpfahl," Zitty, October 1993.
Harald Fricke, "Wieder aus der Natur

Schoepfen", <u>Die Tageszeitung</u>, June 1993.
Harald Fricke, "Richtige Form, Richtige Farbe, im Richtigen Movement," <u>Die Tageszeitung</u>, June 1993.
Gisela Sonnenburg, "Schmauch... Schrie...das Protokoll," <u>Naives Deutschland</u>, June 1993.
Kim Levin, "Best Bets Art," <u>The Village Voice</u>, February 1993.

1992

Kim Levin, "Bets Art," <u>The Village Voice</u>, April 1992.

1990

Peter Kloehn, "A-historical Williamsburg," <u>Artscribe</u>, No. 80, March/April 1990.

1989

<u>Photography of Invention Joshua Smith</u>, Smithsonian Museum Press, Washington DC, 1989.
Vicki Goldberg, "The Real America," <u>American Photographer</u>, December 1989.
"Spring Preview," <u>New York Magazine</u>, September 12, 1989.
Vince Aletti, "Best Bets Photography," <u>The Village Voice</u>, August 1989.
John Welchman, "Turning Japanese," <u>Artforum</u>, No. 27, April 1989.

Books and Catalogues

2010

<u>Cognitive Architecture: From Biopolitics to Noo-politics</u>, Ed. Warren Neidich, Deborah Hauptmann, 010 Press

2009

<u>Lost Between the Extensivity / Intensivity Exchange</u>: The Drawings of Warren Neidich, essays by Lia Gangitano, Freek Lomme and Sven-Olov Wallenstein, Onomatopee, Eindhoven, The Netherlands.

2005

<u>Earthling</u>, essays by Barry Schwabsky and interview by Hans Ulrich Obrist, Pointed Leaf Press, New York, New York.

2003

<u>Blow-up: Photography, Cinema and the Brain</u>, essays by Warren Neidich with introduction by Norman Bryson, D.A.P. and the University of California, Riverside.

2000

<u>Camp O.J.</u>, photographs by Warren Neidich with texts by Charles Steinback, Stephen Margulies and David Hunt, Bayle Art Museum, University of Virginia, Charlottesville, Virginia.

1994

<u>Cultural Residue: Contamination and Decontamination</u>, catalogue with Philip Pocock, Villa Arson, Nice, France.

1993

<u>Unknown Artist</u>, essay by Bodjana Pedjick, Fricke & Schmid.

1991

<u>Historical Intervention</u>, catalogue with David Joslit, M.I.T. List Center, Cambridge, Massachusetts.

1989

<u>American History Reinvented</u>, ed. Steve Dietz, photographs by Warren Neidich with essays by Linda Day, Reinhold Misselbeck, Christopher Phillips, Lew Thomas and John Welchman, Aperture.

Awards, Fellowships and Honors

2008

IASPIS Residency, Stockholm, Sweden

2005

Finalist, Creative Capital Award

2005

Arts Council of England Research Fellowship (with Scott Lash)
British Academy Award (with Jules Davidoff)

2004

ACE-AHRB Arts and Science Research Fellowship
Madrid Abierto Public Sculpture Award (with Elena Bajo)

2003

Light Works Fellowship

2002

Lower Manhattan Cultural Center Studio

1998

MacDowell Foundation

1994-1995

Villa Arson

1993

Kunstlerhaus Bethanian

Warren Neidich
Lost Between the Extensivity /
Intensivity Exchange

Onomatopee 25
ISBN-13: 978-90-78454-26-7

Editors:
Warren Neidich, Christine Elson
and Remco van Bladel

Managing director and exhibition curator:
Freek Lomme for Onomatopee

Text contributions by:
Lia Gangitano, Director of Participant Inc.
and Curatorial Advisor PS 1-MOMA,
New York.
Sven-Olov Wallenstein, philosopher and
editor of the art journal Site.
Freek Lomme, freelance curator and writer,
director of Onomatopee, curator of your-
space/Van Abbemuseum and editor of
art journal De Kantlijn.

Design:
Remco van Bladel

Photography:
Ingmar Swalue (p. 97 - 112)

Printing & lithography:
Die Keure, Brugge, Belgium

Paper:
Go! Matt, 135 gr/m2

Edition:
1000

Acknowledgement:
We would like to thank the following people
who made this work and book possible.

Elena Bajo
Adam Budak
Caroline Donath
EDHV
Christine Elson
IASPIS team, Stockholm
Anke Hamers
Sarrita Hun
Jan Ketz
Barbara Lauterbach
NGBK
Christine Peters
Pro-qm team,
Robert Stasinski
Gabriel Stellbaum
Nina de Wit
Cecilia Widenheim
Axel Wieder

Publisher:
Onomatopee
Kanaalstraat 8
5611 CT Eindhoven
The Netherlands
+31 (0)40 - 202 78 85
info@onomatopee.net
www.onomatopee.net

Distribution:
Idea Books
Nieuwe Herengracht 11
1011 RK Amsterdam
The Netherlands
+31 (0)20 - 622 61 54
idea@ideabooks.nl

This publication appeared partially within
the framework of the collaborative project
'Images and Imagination', a project wherein
two Eindhoven presentation spaces,
Onomatopee and De Overslag, showed
two solo exhibitions of artists dedicated
to issues of visual reception. Onomatopee
presented Warren Neidich, De Overslag presented Yoann van Parys. www.deoverslag.nl

Supported by:
Gemeente Eindhoven / Pokon fund
Delft School of Design